P9-BXX-920

OPERATION
CHRISTMAS CHILD

OPERATION CHRISTMAS CHILD

CHRISTMAS CHILD

A STORY OF SIMPLE GIFTS

FRANKLIN GRAHAM

and Donna Lee Toney

B&H
PUBLISHING GROUP

Nashville, Tennessee

978-1-4336-7999-5

Published by B&H Publishing Group
Nashville, Tennessee

Dewey Decimal Classification: 266.023
Subject Heading: MINISTRY \ OPERATION CHRISTMAS CHILD \
MISSIONS

Unless otherwise noted all Scripture quotations are taken from the
New King James Version, copyright © 1979, 1980, 1982, Thomas
Nelson Publishers, Inc.

Scripture quotations marked NIV are taken from the New International
Version, copyright © 1973, 1978, 1984 by International Bible Society.

Scripture quotations marked NLT are taken from the New Living
Translation, copyright © 1996, 2004, 2007 by Tyndale House
Foundation. Used by permission.

Scripture quotations marked Phillips are taken from J. B. Phillips,
"The New Testament in Modern English", 1962 edition,
published by HarperCollins.

Some names have been changed or withheld
for protection of individuals.

Photographs: Property of Samaritan's Purse; used by permission.

1 2 3 4 5 6 7 8 • 17 16 15 14 13

DEDICATION

A Story of Simple Gifts is dedicated to the Lord's Army of compassionate hearts—our Operation Christmas Child volunteers.

From Asia to Australia, from Europe to the Americas, from the Middle East to Africa, these dedicated men, women, and young people serve with a sense of calling, hearts of compassion, and an overwhelming desire to see children come to know Jesus Christ as their Savior.

From the staff of Samaritan's Purse and the Operation Christmas Child team—and from our many donors who make this work possible—we say thank you and God bless you in your sacrificial service that reaches around the world to the glory of God.

> "Doing the will of God from the heart, with goodwill doing service, as to the Lord, and not to men, knowing that whatever good anyone does, he will receive the same from the Lord." (Eph. 6:6–8)

Preface: On the Outside Wanting In

"What appears to be the thing that young people are looking for the most?" This was a question my father Billy Graham once asked the president of Harvard University. Without hesitation he answered: "They want to belong."

Even children in faraway places have a strong desire to "belong" but do not know why, or to what, or to whom. The Bible tells us that God has set eternity in the hearts of the human race (Eccles. 3:11). Even children search for this great truth—the meaning of life.

This is the purpose of Operation Christmas Child—to proclaim the message that Jesus Christ came to mankind in the form of the Christmas Child, to bring eternal life to all. What a blessing it is when people come to Christ as children. But how can they hear this message without someone to tell them?

The shoebox is the vehicle God has put into our hands to reach the little children of the world. We have seen how receptive children are to the Gospel message and we want to be faithful in proclaiming its great truth—inviting a lost world into the saving faith of the Lord Jesus Christ.

Some years ago, Samaritan's Purse had joined with national church leaders in Kosovo to do a massive shoebox distribution in that war-torn country. Four-wheel drive vehicles loaded with cartons of shoeboxes took the team about twelve miles off the beaten path, back into the hills around Kosovo, a European country in the central part of the Balkan Peninsula. This once-suppressed society allowed Operation Christmas Child to "come in" from what had been to them the "outside world."

The little school was abuzz with excitement when the team arrived. The teachers had prepared the children for a party and they were patiently waiting. As the vehicles approached the schoolhouse, children were halfway out the windows waving. Not to keep them in suspense any longer, the team quickly organized the distribution and handed out hundreds of boxes along with a Gospel storybook for each child.

While the children sang and played together with their toys, and heard the Christmas story, one of the team members walked outside the building and found a little boy standing at the window, peering into the schoolhouse with longing in his eyes.

Many children are forbidden by their parents or guardians to attend a distribution or to accept a gift from strangers, but the longing in their eyes is something not easily forgotten.

There are still many little ones on the outside wanting in, and this is what keeps us motivated—to reach as many as possible with the Gospel that calls lost souls from the world of sin into God's forgiveness and love.

This book, therefore, gives account of Jesus Christ, the Savior of lost souls, who calls people into His salvation. Winning the hearts of children for Him is what keeps us on the journey to deliver a profound message in a simple shoebox.

INTRODUCTION

Christmas! *It's still summertime*, I thought, as I propped my boots up on the desk and listened to the young man calling from England.

Jumping into the Christmas flurry didn't excite me too much, but Christmas in July is a big event in western North Carolina. Mountain towns rope off Main Street lined with booths that are filled with local crafts. Exhibitors peddle homemade tree ornaments. Banners coax residents and vacationers to shop early, even though Christmas is still months away.

Being in ministry nearly forty years has taught me the importance of planning ahead. But in the early days, I embraced each one for what it held in store.

Having just returned from Croatia and Bosnia and soon headed to Somalia and Sudan, Christmas was the furthest thing from my mind. Yet on that summer morning 1993, there was something about what the man said that got my attention—he wanted to help the children of Bosnia who had been left homeless, injured, and hopeless. "Will you help us?" he asked.

It was the height of the war in Bosnia. I had already been there three times that year. Thousands of refugees had been scattered throughout the Balkan states. Husbands and fathers had been killed. Hospitals were filled with young widows and children who had been stricken with multiple injuries. It was a mess!

Samaritan's Purse had provided relief supplies to families that had been torn apart through the atrocity of ethnic cleansing. We had shipped one hundred thousand copies of my father's book *Peace with God* for these victims of war who were longing for peace, giving them the opportunity to read in their own language about God's salvation and finding real peace with Him. We had sent Bible storybooks to comfort children caught in the incomprehensible war.

All of this was going through my mind as the man poured his heart out and shared with me his plan to fill empty shoeboxes with small toys and needed items to deliver to the children of war at Christmastime.

Samaritan's Purse had become proficient in packing and shipping box loads of medicines, cartons of food, containers of equipment and supplies—but shoeboxes? What could possibly fit inside a shoebox that could help anyone in despair? But I couldn't say no.

"I'll be glad to help," I told him and hung up. I stared out the window at the brilliant sun, listened to the sounds of summer, and thought, *Christmas time's a comin'—but it's still a long way off.*

BIG TROUBLE, BIG TASK, BIG THANKS

Days before Thanksgiving my secretary came through the door with a look on her face that I knew very well. "Do you remember that man from Britain that called you back in the summer asking for shoeboxes? He's on the phone asking when you'll be sending them— he's leaving for Bosnia soon," she stated with an air of "You're in big trouble!" I had forgotten about it and now the Christmas season was fast approaching.

I picked up the phone. "Mr. Graham, how many shoeboxes have you collected?" I couldn't let him down. His cause was worthy, so I said, "David, we're working on it; I'll get back to you." He was thrilled and I was, well, in trouble.

"We've got to collect some shoeboxes—fast!" I said. We threw some ideas around and then called Ross Rhoads, a member of our board of directors and, at the time, senior pastor of Calvary Church in Charlotte, North Carolina. As always, Ross was glad to help and said, "Tell me what to do."

"Get a shoebox and fill it with some little toys for kids—maybe some toothpaste and a toothbrush, a hair brush, and socks," I suggested. "Take it to the pulpit on Sunday and show your congregation. Ask if they will help us collect shoebox gifts for the kids in Bosnia. And by the way, tell them to put a note inside with their picture so the child will know who the box is from—maybe some of the kids will write back." Ross enthusiastically agreed. Then I called Sean Campbell, our executive director in Canada. "Sean, see what kind of response you can get from a church up there."

I hung up and forgot about it again, until a few days after Thanksgiving. My secretary walked into my office and announced a call from Ross with that "you're in trouble" look on her face. "Ross needs to talk to you."

Picking up the phone, I heard his voice filled with troubled excitement. "Franklin, you've got to send someone down here to pick up all of these shoeboxes!"

"What do you mean?" I asked.

"Well, we've got shoeboxes stacked up in the gym, in the foyer, and in Sunday school rooms—they're in the way."

"So you've really been able to collect a few hundred boxes?" I asked.

"A few hundred?" Ross answered. "How about eleven thousand!" I was stunned. Ross had a big church, but eleven thousand in two weeks? He said, "Franklin, this is obviously something the Lord has blessed."

Reflecting years later, Ross said, "All I did that Sunday morning was to show the congregation a shoebox Carol had packed and asked them to do the same. That afternoon, a member of the church with the Bible Broadcast Network (BBN) interviewed me and gave me the chance to tell about the project. We did not solicit for boxes nor was the church address given. Over the next several days, however, people began bringing shoeboxes to the church and deliveries were made daily by the post office and courier services. The church was known for 'sending help,' but 'receiving' was not something we were set up for."

I said a great big thank you to Ross and then placed a call to David and reported the big news. Immediately, I sent my projects director (now vice president of projects and government relations)

Kenney Isaacs to Charlotte to assess the situation. He called and said, "Franklin, you're not going to believe this. People are really excited!"

The response was so overwhelming that Ross suggested I come on Sunday, December 12, to preach and thank the congregation.

HYPHENATED BY THE TURN OF THE CENTURY

That was twenty years ago. Two decades have passed—hyphenated by the turn of the century. Not every generation experiences living from one millennium to another. We have now surpassed that milestone and have come into the second decade of the twenty-first century, marking one hundred million shoebox gifts collected and delivered, representing an even larger number who have heard God's message. When I look back on this project—Operation Christmas Child (OCC)—I think of the Scripture that says, "Oh, what God has done!" (Num. 23:23).

The Lord has blessed this outreach in numbers—monumental numbers. But more important, He has blessed it by changing hearts, one at a time. And in the twentieth year of Operation Christmas Child, we delivered the one hundred millionth shoebox!

There are miles of smiles that tell stories about changed lives, miles of oceans away. But it all started with:

One phone call

One request

One shoebox

One church

And one message about the Christmas Child

For one heart at a time

We pray that the heartbeat of the Gospel will stir the hearts of hundreds of millions more.

Come with us on this journey as we tell you about one profound truth that changes one life at a time.

—Franklin Graham

LOOKING BACK WHILE MOVING FORWARD

$\ast$

The year 1993 was a turning point for Samaritan's Purse—and for many people who rummaged through their closets to find shoeboxes just waiting to be filled with something more than shoes! Recycling is a big thing these days and Operation Christmas Child was steps ahead. We put shoeboxes back into circulation—filling them with smiles that would travel miles to children not forgotten by God.

When Ross and Carol Rhoads agreed to help fulfill a promise I had made to David Cooke in England, we could have never guessed what the Lord had in store for our ministry and for children, families, and churches around the world. Many who had never thought about reaching out to their neighbors began engaging with pastors and Christians in countries burdened by Communism, ravaged by war, ruined by natural disasters, or devastated by famine and disease. When we think of people around the world in turmoil, we think of terrorized victims who need to be reached with God's truth, but the churches in these countries had so little to work with.

Like March winds that come in like a lion, the first surprising collection of twenty-eight thousand shoeboxes in the United States and Canada within a two-week period caused OCC to roar into existence and it has been like a runaway train—but one that has kept the course. The years have rushed by and we have marveled at God's great work accomplished through a simple concept—giving a gift that carries a prayer and the Gospel message in the name of Jesus.

The idea of children giving to children electrified families, families got churches excited, and before we knew it, businesses were catching the vision. Like a rocket, the idea spread like wildfire that seemed to burn off the dross of complacency. Whether rich or poor, filling a shoebox seemed a realistic goal for anyone to reach, and the results were dynamite, kindling passionate generosity in people's hearts.

It wasn't long before we saw the reaction from children receiving the boxes. Some opened their shoebox, carefully selected a gift and then handed the box back. When they were told the entire box belonged to them, their joy was indescribable as they peered back into the box with wonder. We see this still today; some cry, others giggle, but most just hug the boxes close to their grateful hearts. For many children in harsh and cruel places, one small present by our standards is unbelievably lavish by another's.

We have been asked over and over, "When are you going to put in a book what God has done through Operation Christmas Child?"

Samaritan's Purse has tried through the years to document how the Lord has blessed this outreach. We have sent out newsletters, special reports, and the always popular videos and DVDs that live up to the integrity that a picture is worth a thousand words. It takes a great library to catalog the photographs and volumes to document the reports. But it takes only one book to whet the appetite in telling how one heart can be changed, one person at a time.

The milestones are worth recounting. The stories are heartwarming and riveting, and the answers to prayer so real. This is what you now hold in your hands. But while this one book casts twenty years into framed memories, it will more importantly point you to the Book that is our foundation—the Bible—God's Holy Word.

THE "PURSE" BEFORE THE BOX

Children are gifts from God and should be valued because they are greatly valued by God. Common to all—we begin life as children. While reviewing the history of Samaritan's Purse "before the box," we came across a newsletter I had written early in 1993.

> From the beginning, Samaritan's Purse has always had a heart for the kids of war, famine, and disaster. They are such innocent victims in these conflicts. Their young eyes have seen unbelievable horrors that can hardly be described. But it is amazing what comfort a simple little toy can bring. A stuffed teddy bear, a doll, or a toy truck can make such a difference.
>
> Samaritan's Purse is not just another relief organization. We are an evangelistic organization—our goal is to reach out to those in need in the name of the Lord Jesus Christ. Wherever He went, He had compassion on those who were hurting—but His compassion was not limited to people's physical needs. The atrocities of war are unimaginable, and in reaching out to others, we want them to know that God loves them and that Jesus Christ is God's Son. "But God demonstrates His own love toward us, in that while we were still sinners, Christ died for us" (Rom. 5:8).
>
> In Bosnia, we continue to ship aid on a regular basis over well-established land routes. This aid includes food, medical equipment and supplies, clothing, Christian literature, toys, blankets, sleeping bags, and other relief items. Whenever we

send shipments, we do it in the name of Christ and we send literature that tells others about Christ.

When Operation Christmas Child entered the picture, it seemed natural to embrace a tool with such potential for child evangelism. That tool is a simple shoebox. We marvel and thank God for using simple things.

THE FIRST OF ONE
HUNDRED MILLION

Everything starts with "the first." The first day of life. The first day of school. The first dollar earned. The first car. The first home. We love to remember "firsts" because they set us on pathways not knowing exactly where they will lead. This is certainly the story of Operation Christmas Child.

One hundred million shoebox gifts is astonishing, but thinking back to the beginning, I can recall the very first shoebox packed, reminding me of how unique each gift is—one hundred million gifts packed in one hundred million ways.

When Ross agreed to help us collect shoeboxes for kids the very first year, it was a new experience for us all. We had never packed a shoebox for a child.

With a short window of time to make this happen, I called our director of communications at the time, Paula Woodring, to ask if she would go shopping. She was accustomed to my spontaneous requests, so she switched gears and headed to the store. A day or two later she presented the very first shoebox carefully packed, sure to bring a smile to a girl and sure to communicate the care and love wrapped up in such a special package.

In the meantime, Carol Rhoads was busy packing the first shoebox in Charlotte to show to the congregation of Calvary Church. Carol is one of those very organized ladies who carefully keeps the right shoes in the right shoebox, so she struggled with which pair of shoes to make "homeless." Pulling a box from the shelf and removing the shoes, she and Ross went to Walmart and filled it with items that would fit inside.

One box for a boy and one box for a girl was all we knew about designating shoeboxes for kids. After the first distribution, we learned that there was much more to this idea.

WILL YOU HELP?

I t is not so easy giving shoebox gifts away. But Kenney began working with Ross's staff to prepare the boxes for shipment and get them out of the church. Trucking companies expressed dismay that we hadn't given them notice of the large numbers of packages needing transport. They had no idea that this had not been planned. Sadly, on our part, it had not been expected. But the Lord answered our prayers by providing shoeboxes for kids, not by human standards, but from the "riches of Heaven." He took the one box that had been presented to the people and multiplied it.

While we were accustomed to logistics of sending aid to foreign countries, we were surprised to learn that these boxes had to be inspected before receiving clearance by US customs. Inspect twelve thousand little boxes?

I was grateful that Kenney happened to be home instead of half-way around the world as he usually was. He had given leadership to our disaster relief efforts and there was no one better than him to bring structure to chaos in the making. Ross invited Kenney to speak to the congregation on a Sunday morning.

"Will you help us?" Kenney asked. "You see, these shoeboxes need to be moved out of your church, but before we can ship them to Bosnia, they have to be inspected and prepared for transport—today!"

That Sunday afternoon, three hundred volunteers from the church showed up in the gymnasium: men, women, teenagers, boys and girls, moms, dads, and grandparents. The excitement was thrilling; the sounds of joy filled the house of God.

Imagine the scene. No preparation had been made. No flyers had been sent out. No time on anyone's calendar had been blocked to do this work. When people got ready for church that morning, they had no idea what lay in store. But God knew. God was there in the hearts of the people. How do we know? Joy—heavenly joy—filled that place. It didn't matter whether they were physicians or pastors, teachers or truck drivers, mothers or machinists, business executives or ball players. Everyone who came on the spur of the moment rolled up their sleeves and set their feet in motion.

But the gym could not hold the boxes and the people. Kenney scrambled to organize processing lines and give on-the-spot training on how to inspect a box of toys. We hadn't thought to instruct people to refrain from packing squirt guns, camouflage clothing, and anything else that resembled war. We didn't think about chocolate melting or liquids spilling out. If boxes were found to contain certain food items, customs would reject the entire box. Kenney assessed the pros and the cons and did all that he could think to do, and the people responded.

One Zero Makes a Huge Difference

"T his idea of a little shoebox gift is huge," Kenney said when he called me from Charlotte. "Franklin, the energy and excitement from Ross's church is something extraordinary. I've never seen anything like this—people are fired up!"

Hearts were ablaze with the love of God that prompted generosity. This was a memorable day—and we learned as we moved forward. Willingness to serve God leads to receiving His guidance every step of the way. I couldn't help but think of the Scripture: "I am the Lord your God . . . who leads you by the way you should go" (Isa. 48:17).

Ross's wonderful church staff and congregation worked tirelessly inspecting the boxes and sealing them with Samaritan's Purse tape. The boxes were stacked on pallets and wrapped in heavy-duty plastic. It was comical to see lopsided pallets because of the variance in shoebox sizes. But the smiles on the faces were "right side up." Happy faces were in abundance.

With the seventeen thousand shoeboxes our Canadian office collected from schools in Calgary, combined with ours, we had a dilemma and had to act with urgency. How will we ship twenty-eight thousand boxes halfway around the world in just a few days?

We contacted USAir asking if they would consider transporting these gifts. At the time we were hopeful we might collect twelve hundred shoebox gifts. The airline had agreed to transport six pallets. But when we learned that we actually had nearly twelve thousand shoebox gifts from the United States alone, we knew it was a long shot to persuade USAir to amend their offer. One zero makes a big difference!

It was going to take an answer to prayer to make this one journey a reality. We prayed that the Lord would open the hearts of the powers that be and grant us favor with more cargo space (at their expense—not ours).

A conference call was made to a woman with USAir, Mrs. May. When she learned that our number had gone from twelve hundred to nearly twelve thousand, she gulped when we asked if the airline would give us more airfreight. As the discussion progressed, prayer was being answered. The call came to a conclusion with her response, "We'll give you the entire load!" Talk about an answer to prayer! Talk about energizing us. Talk about energizing others.

The Christmas spirit also prevailed when Air Canada agreed to ship boxes from Canada to London. These North American airlines worked many hours on our behalf, saving us multiple thousands of dollars in transportation costs.

News outlets had given Samaritan's Purse a tremendous amount of coverage about the relief work we were already doing in Bosnia. Because of worldwide attention to Bosnia at the time, the media attended our press conferences in Charlotte and Calgary, which heightened public awareness of the project. The coverage sparked enthusiasm that invigorated people to "come and help us."

Not until the boxes took flight did we realize the far-reaching impact that one simple gift could carry the Gospel abroad in a simple cardboard box.

GOING IN JESUS' NAME

Surprised by the response, our offices in Boone and Calgary were hopping as we worked through the details of getting the boxes to Europe. Our office in London was helping organize truck convoys to transport the boxes into Croatia and Bosnia.

Samaritan's Purse had infrastructure and management in place to handle on-the-ground operations. But because of the shortness of time, we jumped over every hurdle that presented itself, mobilizing every resource we had from churches and pastors, from missionaries and volunteers, to freight companies and government agencies. Anyone and everyone who could and would help, we contacted. To pull this off in a matter of days was impossible, but not with the Lord.

My calendar was already full so I wasn't able to travel to Bosnia. It was important that the venture have spiritual leadership, so I prevailed upon Ross once again. "Will you lead a team to Bosnia to distribute these gifts?" Ross was not only a close friend; he was the vice chairman of my board of directors, a pastor with a heart for children, and an evangelist himself with a passion for the lost. Ross knew that he and Carol would be entering a danger zone by going into Bosnia, but without hesitation he said, "Of course we'll go." And they did.

This first delegation experienced the joy that a simple shoebox can bring to one boy, one girl. I told Ross that I would send with him a capable team of individuals who, by themselves, were brave souls with accomplished Christian service. They could maneuver obstacles with God's help.

Kenney joined the Rhoads along with Sean, who had previously served as a missionary in the killing fields of Cambodia. I called my directors in London, David Applin, an Anglican pastor, and Jean

Wilson, whom I tagged with the title "Queen Jean." She was a stout lady who adequately held an enormous heart of compassion; she had worked for my father since the 1960s. Stan Barrett, Hollywood stunt man and first to break the on-land sound barrier in a rocket car in 1979, also went along. Believe me, this crowd didn't scare easily.

Others were part of this group I tagged the Red Team, and gave them all red jackets to easily keep track of one another. The truth was that red represented many things: danger, sacrifice, courage, and passion. I knew they were going into a dangerous war zone. I knew they were making sacrifices to be away from their families during the Christmas season. I knew they each had passion for lost souls and compassion for the weary. And I knew that they would go in the name of Jesus Christ, the fearless One, who would strengthen them with courageous love.

THE RED TEAM

The Red Team assembled for the first time in Zagreb at a European hotel that had been hit multiple times with rocket fire. They gathered for a time of prayer and mobilization at 5:00 the next morning.

A convoy of small vehicles that had endured the effects of war became the caravan that took them to Split, the largest Dalmatian city on the eastern shores of the Adriatic Sea.

Later that day they headed to Mostar—named after the bridge keepers who, in medieval times, guarded the Stari Most, the Old Bridge built by the Ottomans in the sixteenth century. It is one of the most recognizable landmarks in the Balkan states. It also happened to be a very dangerous part of the city.

Still, the Red Team made its way to a school where they were greeted by children who had been all but forgotten. Mostar had been divided into the western part dominated by the Croat forces, and the eastern part where the Army of the Republic of Bosnia and Herzegovina had driven large numbers of the population from their homes.

In route, they came to a derailed train that had been abandoned. Families who had been run out of their homes by the fighting found refuge there and were living inside the box cars.

Compelled to stop, the team did a spontaneous distribution. The response from the box car villagers was indescribable as children hugged their gifts, mothers cried with joy, and the few fathers that had survived the fighting struggled to convey their deep thanks for bringing joy to their little ones.

The caravan then continued on. Door-to-door combat and shelling was evident by the cracks of gunfire and explosions filling the air. Danger lurked.

Kenney kept a close eye on everyone. He had taken as many flak jackets as we could round up in such short notice. Assessing the situation, he waved the vehicles to the roadside and insisted everyone suit up. He gave Queen Jean his flak jacket to add to the one she already had on. Respectfully speaking, Jean was a strappin' lady and Kenney wanted to make sure that she was protected.

Jean, with the capable help of her longtime assistant Pat Strange, had been hard at work collecting boxes in London and she was thrilled to be among the first to distribute the boxes. Always the proper lady, Jean traveled to Bosnia in her belted dress, pearl beads and high-heel pumps. The added ninety pounds of steel weight did not affect her as she climbed into the tiny vehicle with a mischievous smile on her face. I remember Kenney telling me later, "Franklin, I wish you could have seen Jean crammed into that little car, barely able to move." But I knew Jean Wilson—forever content.

With all that settled, the Red Team continued on—speeding through Sniper Alley. For Stan Barrett—the rocket car man—he was in his element.

Artillery exploded in the distance as the team arrived at the hospital. Quickly stacking the boxes on gurneys, they rolled them through the corridors. Part of the hospital had been winged off due to massive destruction and the team was guided through the wards under watchful eyes. But when they encountered the children, the only eyes that mattered to them were those of the little patients.

Good logistics and lots of prayer had gotten the team this far, now compassion stepped in and the evidence of answered prayer was clearly seen. There could have been no better representatives than Ross and Carol Rhoads, whose spiritual leadership was empowered by the Holy Spirit that day. What came to the surface was verification that the shoebox gift was most certainly a tool in God's hand. While we intended this to be a one-time project to help children in Bosnia, we knew that we had to contemplate expanding this program into the future—and sure enough—God led us into exciting possibilities that could have only come through His guiding hands.

MY LIFE STARTED WHEN I WAS TWELVE

$\ast$

The impact a shoebox made in a child's life is all it took to realize that Operation Christmas Child was going to be around for a long time. Lejla Allison's account comes as full circle as any because she received a shoebox in 1993, the first year we embarked on the journey to Bosnia. Today, twenty years later, she packs boxes and serves as an OCC full circle speaker.

"My life really started when the man from America handed me the box," Lejla said. "Before that, I just existed. That was twenty years ago. So while I may be thirty-two now, I'm really no older than OCC, because after meeting the Christmas Child—the Lord Jesus Christ—I found life."

Born to impoverished parents, Lejla was just twelve years old when she received her first gift and heard about Jesus for the first time. If any American city had experienced a December snowfall of five feet, no school would have been open. But on that frosty morning in Bosnia, Lejla's mother woke her, dressed her, and put an old pair of shoes on her feet. The toes of the shoes were ripped open. Her father had tried to close them up with steel wire but the leather was so rotten it wouldn't hold together. Lejla's mother wrapped her feet in bags and sent her out into the arctic chill that defines Balkan winters.

A bulldozer had come through early that morning and cleared a narrow path in the road that remained slippery and messy. Lejla may have been walking toward the school five miles away, but she had no intention of showing up there. If ever an adolescent was on the brink of giving up, it was Lejla. To prove it, she purposely detoured into a landmine field where just the day before her best friend had been killed and another friend had lost his leg in an explosion. *Maybe if she walked through the same field she could end her miserable life. She had no reason to live. With no coat to keep her warm, maybe she would even die from the frigid temperatures,* she thought. She was tired of being cold, weary of hunger pains, and afraid of the future. She knew that within two years her parents would give her away in marriage, according to tradition—it happened to all girls once they reached the eighth grade. "The horror was so real," she said, "that I felt my soul being ripped from me."

Lejla had been taught that their god existed to punish people. "Why?" Lejla had asked her parents. "Why does life have to be so cruel?" They answered, "Because we are sinners and this is our god's punishment for us. We must pay for the sins of Adam and Eve and there is nothing we can do about it. We cannot hope for any good. If we work hard to do good things, we may find salvation."

Lejla had no reason to doubt her parents. "All around me," Lejla said, "was the evidence that the god we worshiped offered no hope, no other way. Men were exalted and women were property. If I had questioned this, there would have been severe consequences. But in my own heart, I wondered why any god could want this for me? It didn't seem right. I cried out, 'God, if you have any mercy, could you forgive me of the terrible sin and show me your mercy?'"

After forty-five minutes of wandering through the landmine field with no answers and no explosion, Lejla looked into the sky and cried, "God, I hate you for hating me so much and wanting me to suffer like this. If you think I'm going to live like this, I'll show you." Then she headed toward Sniper Alley with the certainty it promised; one hundred percent guarantee of being shot to death. She slipped under the barricade and wrenched her neck up toward the mountains, waiting for a powerful boom to end her misery. It didn't happen.

I found myself walking toward the school, disappointed I had survived Sniper Alley. As I approached, I saw some kids holding boxes and I wondered where they had gotten them. We had nothing new; even primitive items were scarce. As I got closer, I noticed how bright and beautiful the boxes were. One of the boys said, "There are people inside giving these away. You can get one too."

Why do I need a box? Lejla thought. *I don't have anything to put in it. It's pretty, but it won't do me any good.* When I walked inside, I saw an older gentleman sitting on the steps. He jumped up and grabbed a box from the top of the pile and headed toward me. But I didn't want any interaction. I wanted to be left alone. I was bitter and hateful. To make matters worse, the man had a big smile on his face and gently said, "I want you to have this." I took it so he would go away quickly, but to my surprise the box was not empty. The heaviness caused my hands to give way slightly. I took hold, turned and ran as fast as I could until I found a solitary corner and slumped to the floor, cradling the box in my lap. My heart was racing and my emotions were fragile. Do I dare hope for what might be inside? After all, this is a shoebox. I looked down at my frozen feet, and then with great apprehension, lifted the lid. Inside was a pair of brand new sneakers.

For some time I sat and cried while lifting the lid and then closing it. The crying had left me weak and quivering. I felt sick, then happy. As I drew the sneakers out of the box, my hands bumped into other things. The shoes that fit perfectly were enough, but more?

I pulled out a twelve pack of pencils. My entire class of fifty-eight students had been sharing a nub of one pencil all year long, and now I had my very own! A notebook was there to replace the one I had used for three years, with hardly scribble space left. Then I discovered erasers that smelled like strawberries—the first smell of anything pleasant that I could remember. We had grown accustomed to gun powder and decaying bodies. When I clasped a tube of toothpaste, I opened and tasted it. The flavor was so delicious that I nearly ate it all. Energized by the thrill, I gathered my new belongings and got home as fast as I could, hoping that none of the kids would steal my box from me on the way.

My mother was stunned when I came through the door and inquired where I had gotten all of my treasures. "A man gave them to me and said the box was from Jesus" I assumed there was someone in America by that name. That night, I pulled out my new pen and notebook and wrote a letter to Jesus, telling Him things I had never told anyone.

At school the next day, I found the man who had given me the box and asked him if he would take the letter to America and give it to Jesus. He explained that Jesus was God's Son and that He came to pay the penalty for man's sin. This was so different from what I had heard. He told me that Jesus is the One who died for our sins and that if I confessed my sin to Him, Jesus would forgive me and love me as His very own. The man spoke truth to me and I had no reason to doubt him, for I already knew that He had heard and answered my prayer. He was real and I knew He had mercy. I realized that God was not the god I was told to fear.

At first, my parents thought it was a phase that would pass, but in time, they saw my life and attitude change and this was something that was staying with me. They threatened me and said to give Jesus up. When I wouldn't, physical punishment was executed. When that didn't work, they were ready to take necessary steps to stop my obsession with Him.

I remember coming home with Bible pages that a friend had given me hidden inside my homework papers. I loved the book of Matthew and would read and study the verses. I hid the Word of God in my heart and realized that the more I talked about Him, the more consequences would come. God's protective hand spared me the horrors of an arranged marriage and teenage motherhood. Instead, I was led along a pathway He designed for me.

In Jesus' wonderful way, He reached down from Heaven into a little girl's frightened heart and saved me, and He used a shoebox to do this miracle in my life. Today, I may not have the physical possessions that filled my shoebox that day, but I have the most valuable and lasting possession—eternal salvation and assurance that my soul belongs to Him.

To make it sweeter, He allowed me to come to America and personally say *"hvala"* (thank you) to all those Christians who make the shoebox ministry possible. I have my own family now and we are privileged to pack fifteen hundred shoeboxes each year. If only one person finds salvation through these boxes, my life will have been worthwhile. I am among the one hundred million souls that have been touched by Operation Christmas Child, and changed by the Jesus of Heaven and Earth who reached out to me.

THE HEART OF THE PROJECT

S tories like this tenderize the heart, raise the awareness of the need for the Gospel, and call God's people to "come and help." So as we rolled into 1994, we spent a good bit of time considering our part in the shoebox program. While I am all for doing what is possible to alleviate suffering, following biblical principles of helping others for the purpose of sharing the love of Christ and His Gospel message fuels the work of Samaritan's Purse. My primary concern was not could we collect boxes, but rather if we could ensure that the Gospel would be the heart of the project.

Based on the story that Jesus told of the Good Samaritan in Luke 10, I knew that the only way our involvement in this mission would be fruitful was to put Jesus Christ at the very center. The parable that the Lord told of the man left for dead along the roadside was to teach the ministry of mercy. Jesus is the Merciful One. His great and abundant mercy was evidenced on the cross when He shed His blood to redeem mankind from sin. If people would only stop to listen and receive Him, souls would receive His mercy.

This was the challenge before us; I knew there was ministry potential in the shoebox concept. I invited David Cooke and his colleague Dai Hughes to Boone. We discussed deepening the purpose of collecting and distributing the boxes. We learned that they were struggling to raise the needed funds to sustain the project as it was structured. They readily admitted that they did not have the resources and infrastructure to continue nor had they made an attempt to minister to the children. Their work was humanitarian in purpose, without a plan to utilize the boxes as evangelistic tools. Our friends in England eventually bowed out and asked us to continue the project.

We mutually agreed that we would promote the project and give it a biblical foundation. We began formulating a structure that would make Operation Christmas Child a project of Samaritan's Purse, not only in the United States, and Canada, but throughout the United Kingdom (UK), Germany, and Australia. These would become our primary sending countries.

THE PARKING LOT VISIT

Our hands were full. With massive commitments around the world, I needed Kenney in too many other places. We began praying that God would send someone who could help us with Operation Christmas Child to develop a plan of working with, and through, the body of Christ—the church.

We had many capable people on staff, but to find someone who could work with churches and suppliers was a tall order. It is always rewarding to wait on the Lord, but waiting is not fun. Most of us are impatient by nature. I like things to happen fast. I have learned, however, that running ahead of the Lord produces regret because we miss His best. So while praying, I admit that I wasn't expecting such a person to literally knock at our door.

Exactly one year from the infamous call from London, I had an impromptu meeting in the parking lot of Samaritan's Purse that led us a little further down the road in developing our "shoebox department."

On July 4, 1994, I pulled up to the front entrance of my office and was met by a sharp young couple who had stopped to get a look at our operation. The young man introduced himself and his wife, and told me of his interest in Samaritan's Purse. Todd and Kim Chasteen had been in town for the holiday. I learned that he was a nonprofit tax attorney who worked for a friend of mine in Charlotte. After a brief visit, I gave him directions through the mountains to the fireworks scheduled that evening. Before leaving, he gave me his card.

I gave the card to our executive vice president the next day and asked him to make contact with Todd, inviting him back for a preliminary interview. Still puzzled as to why an attorney with a prestigious firm would be interested in moving to Boone to help us, his desire seemed sincere.

The more I began to consider the benefits of having an attorney work with us full time, it didn't seem like such a crazy idea. After all, we consulted frequently with attorneys because the tax laws for nonprofits were fluid. We also had issues with our international offices from time to time and keeping up with international law was a challenge.

Todd returned several days later and we spent more time together. I was impressed with his heart for ministry and told him that we might have a need for his services. His response was interesting: "I don't have to do legal work for you; I'll just serve the Lord in any capacity."

I hadn't considered that possibility. Why waste talent and experience? I had learned that if people are misplaced they don't thrive. Yet, I had a hard time reconciling whether Samaritan's Purse was ready for its own legal counsel.

Todd's heart for ministry was evident to me and I began to see that God was answering prayer. Perhaps Todd could help us with the shoeboxes. After all, most of the disciples were fishermen by trade, but they left all to be fishers of men. Why shouldn't Todd have that opportunity, especially if that was how God was leading?

I told Todd the sequence of events the past year and how God had obviously blessed. He was excited, wanting to know what plan was in place as we moved forward.

"Plan?" I asked. "We just want to be obedient to the Lord. If we continue with this project, its purpose has to be to work with the churches and win children to Jesus. Right now the program is lacking these vital elements," I explained. "Who knows, maybe we'll collect a million boxes someday," I said. "Will you come and help us?"

Todd smiled. Within days, Todd and Kim moved to Boone one month after our introduction, and one year after the call from England.

WHY NOT A MILLION NOW?

Todd jumped in with both feet. He has said since then that he was so naive about the challenges ahead he silently thought we might even collect a million boxes by Christmas. It was already August.

Serving as director for the project domestically under Kenney, Todd took on his first challenge—putting together a list of churches and sending information packets about the project asking, "Will you help us?" Todd thought this would be a fairly easy endeavor. *Who wouldn't want to be involved in such an exciting program?* he thought. But he learned quickly that it wasn't such an easy task.

We knew that churches generally supported their own mission programs, with little to no interaction between denominations. They were not open to parachurch organizations coming in with their own ministry programs. I understood this; yet if pastors heard what God was doing it could inspire, and perhaps even boost, their own mission programs.

Packets were printed, assembled, and mailed to sixty-seven churches in the fall. Many responded that they were not interested in taking on another program—especially at Christmastime. Instead of being discouraged though, we were thankful for the few churches that enthusiastically came on board.

Approximately fifteen churches in four cities became our start-up base: Charlotte, Atlanta, Dallas, and Los Angeles/Orange County. Board members and senior pastors Skip Heitzig of Calvary Chapel of Albuquerque, New Mexico, and Greg Laurie of Harvest Christian Fellowship of Riverside, California, led the way in igniting enthusiasm for the project in their churches that spread across other western cities. Jack Graham, senior pastor of Prestonwood Baptist Church in Dallas, Texas, mobilized church members to help us.

Todd was working diligently for sponsorships—one being air freight. USAir had committed to help us again, but we had to establish a base of operation that could handle what we were praying for—more boxes than the year before.

Through friendly negotiations, Todd solidified a partnership with Panalpina Group, one of the world's leading providers of air freight. The closest base of operation was Huntsville, Alabama. We were able to secure warehouse space there and that became our first processing center (PC) which included a small office and an incoming mail room overseen by Bryan Willis (who also ran our mail operation in Boone). Bryan, now our director of special events, was critical to this endeavor because Samaritan's Purse has always been careful to secure donations along with names and addresses to insure proper acknowledgement and receipting.

Todd began recruiting people and vendors to come and help in each area. Utilizing volunteers was new territory for us and certainly for Todd, but his legal background was invaluable to us as we entered into agreements with various service providers. He was a good negotiator and people easily liked him.

We had a small base of church support in Huntsville and a little band of media, but it was not the hub of operation for our ministry. The ladies who managed the warehouse helped in many ways, even recruiting several members of the United Auto Workers. They seemed out of their comfort zone; nevertheless, we couldn't have done it that year without them.

We scheduled a press conference in Huntsville and had carefully staged the event intending to have a cargo plane in the background, canvassed with a massive banner: OPERATION CHRISTMAS CHILD. As time neared, we learned the plane was running late. Kenney and Todd scrambled and found another airline nearby whose management graciously moved one of their craft into position to stand in for the plane still in the sky. Thankfully, it finished well. More important, we learned how "not" to do a press conference.

BACK TO THE PARKING LOT!

The media in Charlotte was good to us. Our press event was well covered and generated a lot of interest, excitement, and participation. We felt at home in North Carolina surrounded by our donors and many churches that were catching the vision of what we were trying to do. The media was intrigued.

Todd's wife Kim had been the public relations director at the airport before moving to Boone and was able to connect Todd to Al Beamon, the USAir hangar director. He and his team made it possible for us to hold the press event in the hangar. We assembled the children on stage with shoeboxes stacked high. Planes roaring overhead did not drown out the buzz of excitement—it was electrifying. *USA Today* published a positive article afterward, accompanied by a great photo capturing the event that gave us exposure we could have never bought. More prayers answered.

USAir had come through for us again in donating airfreight, and Christmas boxes were once again headed to Bosnia. I threw Ross Rhoads a bit of a curve when I called and asked, "Will you help me again this year and lead a team back to Bosnia?"

"Of course," he said enthusiastically. I told him who would accompany him, and also about the surprise visitor that had thrown a spark of "Americana" into a global story.

"Now Ross, I've invited a little mountain woman from West Virginia to join the team this year," I began.

"Sure—okay," Ross said. But he could sense there was more to the story.

Days before, we had celebrated Thanksgiving. I was glad to have a day at home with my wife, Jane Austin, and our three boys and daughter. The office had been a flurry of activity up until the night before Thanksgiving, so we were enjoying being at home.

The late autumn air was carrying the smell of wood burning through the hollers. A gentle wind blew the brilliant maple leaves to the ground and swirled them around my ankles on my way to the barn. Grabbing an ax, I began chopping a supply of firewood for the winter.

My work came to an abrupt halt when one of the boys ran out to tell me there was a call. Relishing the peacefulness of the outdoors, I didn't care much about talking on the phone and shrugged the message off. But when I looked toward the house, Jane Austin was standing at the door waving me inside.

Grumbling a little, I leaned the ax up against the woodpile, brushed the sawdust off my hands, and headed to the kitchen. While my office was officially closed for the holiday, the receptionist was there handling phone calls that typically came even on holidays.

"There's a woman out in the parking lot with some shoeboxes for you," Jean Smitherman said. I told her I was busy and asked that she have the woman leave the boxes in the lobby.

"You really should come and meet her," she said. Jean whom we all affectionately call "Mama Jean," had worked with us for many years. I knew she wouldn't insist if it didn't seem important.

Sighing, I climbed into the pickup and drove the short distance to the office. Turning into the parking lot, exactly where I had met Todd a few months before, I noticed a truck with a West Virginia license plate and thought, *Surely this woman didn't drive all the way down here today!*

Inside the lobby, Jean pointed toward the family looking at pictures in the hallway. I walked over and introduced myself to this lady who couldn't have weighed ninety pounds, soaking wet.

HARD WORK THE HILLBILLY WAY

"Brother Graham, I'm Mary. Gotcha some shoeboxes fer God. Where do you want 'em?"

"Well, thank you Mary," I said. "Why don't you just leave them here in the foyer? We'll stack them up against the wall."

"Gotcha twelve hundred."

My eyes bulged. "Twelve hundred?" I said, and recalled that was the number we had hoped for the year before—from one church. Here was a collection of twelve hundred from one lady.

"Well, my goodness, Mary. Don't leave them here! Let's take them to the warehouse."

Sure enough, she had driven to Boone that day in a borrowed thirty-foot, twenty-ton panel truck. As they followed me to the warehouse I thought, *Life would sure be dull if we didn't encounter characters from time to time. Mary was one of those endearing characters who make lasting impressions.*

Her son, a stocky young man, backed the truck up to the loading dock. Mary, her husband Ted, son Tad, and youngest daughter Ashley began pulling boxes from the truck faster than I could count them. They would toss several down to me, and I would stack them inside the warehouse. Watching Mary's enthusiasm made me feel like I was helping Santa unload his sleigh.

I kept wondering how she collected so many gifts. Where could anyone find that many shoeboxes in the first place? I watched as she directed her family bouncing in and out of that truck and thought, *This lady has something special! Maybe I should invite her to go with us to Bosnia in a couple of weeks; bet she could help put these shoeboxes in the right hands.*

I initially dismissed the thought, figuring she had never heard of Bosnia. Besides, she might be insulted if I invited her to go into a war zone.

Still, I have always been the impulsive type. "Mary," I said, "how did you hear about this project?"

"I was watchin' the television and saw you talk on Brother Paul and Sister Jan's show. Didn't catch the whole thing, but when you said you needed shoeboxes fer God, I went out and gotcha some."

"But how'd you get twelve hundred?"

Her son grinned proudly as she told the story. "I went up and down the hollers, tellin' everybody that Brother Graham needed shoeboxes fer God. I went to the churches and told them Brother Graham needed boxes filled with gifts fer the chillun in Boze-ne-a. And, Brother Graham, I gotcha some, didn't I?"

"Bless your heart, Mary, you sure did." She continued telling me how she had been inspired to help us after my appearance on TBN with Jan Crouch who has supported OCC from the beginning. Mary told her daughter Muffy, "This is something we can do." I learned later that Muffy had borrowed an old typewriter and as Mary dictated, her daughter typed up a little flyer. They got into their pickup truck and distributed the notices to homes scattered through the hollers, asking neighbors from near and far to help with items for shoeboxes.

Now they didn't have shoeboxes, mind you. As Mary said, "We don't wear shoes much in the hills." Mary's husband Ted began collecting pieces of cardboard from dumpsters and brought them home and cut out a pattern that he used to make shoeboxes, securing each one with miner's tape. Then Mary and the family filled each box with items in response to her request.

I stood there not believing what I was hearing or seeing. Who would think a poor little lady, who hardly had a dime to her name, would go out into impoverished coal mining towns to collect gifts for poor people in Bosnia? I was impressed that she wasn't limited by her own need. Instead, she spent her time trusting the Lord and challenging others to give.

That year she collected more shoeboxes for children in Bosnia than any other single individual; 1,256 to be exact! Her accomplishment was doubly impressive in that she had not solicited these shoeboxes from the wealthy suburbs of big cities—she had gathered them from people who were living in poverty themselves.

The account in Scripture that came to mind was when the apostle Paul said, "Their abundance of joy and their deep poverty overflowed into the wealth of their generosity . . . on their own, according to their ability and beyond their ability, they begged us insistently for the privilege of sharing in the ministry" (2 Cor. 8:2–4 HCSB).

HAVE YOU EVER BEEN TO BOSNIA?

M ary, how would you like to go with us to Bosnia to help give these boxes away?" I couldn't brush the impulse away.

"I'll go."

She answered so quickly that I wasn't sure she understood me; did she realize what kind of place I was talking about? Maybe she didn't know that the country was embroiled in a nasty civil war.

"Ever been to Bosnia?" I asked.

"Nope."

"Ever been overseas?"

"Nope."

"You know, they're shootin' over there. There's a war going on. Got a bulletproof vest?"

"What fer? I got the Holy Spirit of God, young man." She waved her hand in the air. "I've got holy angels all around me, the Spirit of God in me, and Jesus walking with me every step of the way. I'll be alright!"

Her eyes got real big, as if she could see the angels in the air. The tone in her voice picked up the rhythm of an old-time gospel preacher.

I smiled at her depth of faith. "Believe me, Mary," I said, "you'll be just fine."

When I told Ross the story over the phone, I said, "Ross, this is not just some little lady from the hills. She's some kind of woman!"

"Well," Ross said with a little candor, "Carol and I look forward to meeting her and we'll take good care of her." And they did.

Mary had never traveled abroad. We secured a passport for her and sent her a ticket. She flew to Atlanta and miraculously found her way through the largest international airport in the world. She described the transit system inside the terminal as "a wall that opens up inside a train, with a voice that tells you how to get on and where to get off." Mary, with common sense smarts, followed instruction without missing a beat.

On Christmas Eve, shortly after the Rhoads arrived home from Bosnia, I called Ross again. "How did our friend from West Virginia do?"

With the graciousness he's known for, Ross said, "Franklin, she was a blessing. She put her arms around those kids; she prayed with them, she cried with them, she touched them with such tenderness. At times, she even acted like one of them, and they loved her! The Bosnian people really took to her—and so did all the team. She did just great!"

People from her neck of the woods in Ikes Fork, West Virginia, call her Mury (Mary) Damron. She may have come from a poor house in the holler, but within a year's time she would be headed to the White House.

The Blind Boy Sees with His Heart

Have you ever seen a hospital gurney rolling through the corridors piled high with brightly wrapped packages?

You might say this was the team's sleigh. While on the phone with Ross, he told me about some of their experiences. They had paid a visit to the children's cancer ward at a hospital in Zagreb. The shoeboxes had been put into the hands of the children and the gurney was rolling along nearly empty. Ross and Carol stepped into the last ward where a nurse pointed them to an eleven-year-old boy. He had been blinded by shrapnel and had been unresponsive for weeks. "Is there anything you can do?"

Ross and Carol looked at each other and then stepped out into the hallway near the gurney. "What can we give a blind child?" they asked. "He won't be able to see anything." Carol said, "Ross, can we pray?" Immediately, they laid their hands on the remaining boxes and prayed, "Lord, You know this boy's need. Would You give him spiritual sight so that he knows You care for him? Help us to select just the right box where surely there will be something that will open his heart. Amen."

Picking up one of the larger boxes, Ross walked to the boy's bed. Through an interpreter, Ross explained why they had come—that people in America and Canada had packed gifts as an expression of God's great love. The boy seemed unresponsive. Ross tried to guide him to open the box. Still no reaction. Ross finally lifted the lid; his heart racing, "Lord, please let there be something that will break through."

Always a master wordsmith, Ross couldn't speak when he saw the Walkman cassette player with a headset. He lifted it out of the box, installed the batteries, inserted a Christian tape also from the box, and tenderly positioned the headphones over the boy's ears, then clicked the player on.

There was instantaneous reaction. The boy smiled; then his eyes began to move. He responded with great joy. Those standing around were rejoicing because God had answered so specifically.

A Shoebox Big Enough for Booties

This wasn't the only miracle in a shoebox that day. While Ross was in the children's ward, Carol was asked to visit the maternity ward. A young woman, recently widowed due to the war, had been left empty-handed until she gave birth to twins, a boy and a girl.

The shoeboxes are not packed for adults, so Carol felt a little stressed wondering what she could find for a new mother. Then she remembered a very large box on the gurney minutes before. It had stood out to her not because of its size, but because of its crude wrapping. Unlike the others that were brightly colored, this boot box was simply covered in brown wrinkled paper, tied with a shredded rope. The box had remained on the gurney because no one wanted to present an unsightly package to a child.

By the time Carol got back to the gurney, it was gone. She began a mission to find that box and went from floor to floor, describing it to others. Someone emerged with the box and placed it in Carol's hands. She headed back to the ward and prayed that there would be something to encourage this mother's heart.

With the help of an interpreter, Carol told the woman how the box had been packed by people who cared for those who had been deeply affected by war. With bated breath, Carol watched as the gift was unwrapped. What lay inside was a shocking contrast to the outside wrapping; brand new layettes: one pink, one blue; beautifully crocheted bonnets, blankets, and sleepers with all the trimmings—including baby booties.

To this day, Carol cannot tell the story without blinking back tears and thanking the Lord for such a specific answer to prayer. We can just imagine what that young mother must have felt to hold such a gift in her hands.

There's no doubt in my mind that these gifts were designed, directed, and delivered through the power of God. These demonstrations helped us grasp the reality that these shoeboxes carried miracles from the heart of God.

There were many other stories that confirmed that God was in this. His generous arm had been extended to these victims of war. His comfort had reached the brokenhearted of the Balkan states. The gifts had been packed by Christians, but they were given in the name of Jesus. Glory filled the hearts of the packers and presenters, and the Gospel seed was sown into the hearts of the broken.

From that day forward, there was no question that God had guided one giver to fill one box with just the right things that would go to a specific person. This was one time, however, that the number "one" would not be associated with this effective outreach—because this had become more than a one-time program. One empty shoebox sent with prayer and filled with God's love had left behind a spade of blessings in our hearts.

THE DISASTROUS
DISTRIBUTION

While one team was in Bosnia, another team had gone to Rwanda with shoeboxes in response to the brutal massacre that had taken place in July 1994.

Samaritan's Purse had "boots on the ground" days after the news broke. Children by the thousands became orphans, homeless and roaming the countryside. While our intent was not to get into managing facilities, we could not turn our backs on the children left alone in their very cruel world. We opened an orphanage that was the site of our first distribution in Rwanda. We had also reestablished the Central Hospital of Kigali and our team visited the children there also.

Kenney had been in Rwanda a lot that year. We had a strong team on the ground days before Christmas. Todd and Sean had actually traveled to Rwanda aboard a Panalpina cargo jet. They laugh about it now, but at the time I am sure they wondered how they had managed to find themselves traveling not as coach passengers, but as cargo freight!

Canadian radio host Dave Rutherford of QR77 and Gordon Legge of the Calgary Herald had been instrumental in getting word out in western Canada about the collection of shoebox gifts. They were anxious to experience the distribution firsthand. They plopped down inside the cargo plane with the guys. The carrier eventually accommodated them by placing some seats at the rear of the plane, behind the cargo bay. One of the few amenities was the offer of blankets; they shivered all the way to Kigali.

I had asked Skip and Lenya Heitzig to lead the distribution team. Lenya recalled, "Landing in Kigali was eerie—the country had no security or government in place and bandits roamed freely. Kigali, the capital city, was like a ghost town. Windows in the airport terminal had been pierced by bullets. It was not an easy trip. It was not a safe trip. But we never regretted going."

They met the rest of the team at the Canadian consulate. Surgeon Dr. Richard Furman, his wife Harriet, and their daughters Tricia and Holly had joined the team, bringing with them Dr. Walt Harber and his daughters. The Furmans were experienced travelers and Dick, a close friend of mine, board member and cofounder of World Medical Mission, had served in some of the remote mission hospitals around the world. But Dick said, "Rwanda was unlike anything I'd ever seen."

I have always said that it isn't easy to "give things away" to another country. The red tape is "sticky," to say the least. The regulations, the customs, the logistics, the weather, the remote locations, the abrupt and last minute changes, can all spell disaster. Add to that the lack of planning, out of sheer ignorance, makes for the potential of bedlam.

Had it not been for Kenney's keen eye, experience—and most important—God's overseeing hand, our distribution in Kigali would have turned into a riot. Why? Consider what your living room looks like after all the gifts are opened on Christmas morning. Consider the pandemonium created by toddlers, children, and teens almost hyperventilating as they tear into their packages.

Now imagine a little church, the site of a shoebox distribution. Children, who didn't understand the concept of receiving gifts or standing in line, scaled the walls and tried to climb through windows, just wanting to catch a glimpse of a mountain of brightly colored packages that they hoped to hold in their hands.

These children's lives have been turned inside out. They were homeless, dirty, hungry, thirsty, and sick. The only action they had seen the past year was brutality, murder, rape, and the ugliness of ethnic cleansing—things children simply cannot grasp. All of the sudden foreigners appeared with boxes, lots of happy boxes.

That day the team planned to hand out three thousand shoebox gifts. We didn't know how many children would really come, but the team figured there were more boxes than needed. They thought they could keep it organized by controlling how many kids were allowed into the church at a time. But outside, the crowd swelled. The troops were restless and children swarmed the building. The adults, somewhat responsible for the kids, were gathered, watching the indescribable sight.

The kids were grateful, yes, but they were also filled with panic from the excitement and thrill. The team managed to complete the distribution that day and could only hope that all the children had received something.

This was a defining distribution for us because we learned the potential of what can happen. Disaster can erupt even out of good intentions. Todd said later that it was the most exhilarating distribution he has ever experienced, but admitted that he was judging it only by the joy on the children's faces. Kenney, on the other hand, saw the potential for calamity and coined the experience our "disastrous distribution!"

MUSIC TO CALM HER FEARS

"There are no devils left in Hell. They are all in Rwanda," read *Time* magazine's cover story. I had traveled to Byumba, Rwanda, earlier that year and had witnessed the cruel hatred of men. If any place on earth could resemble Hell, Rwanda was it.

While the story is not simple, the civil war in Rwanda boiled down to ethnic fighting between the Hutus and the Tutsis.

This horrific conflict left children orphaned. As the Tutsis were fleeing enemy territory, they would come upon small children sitting beside the decaying corpses of their parents. Escaping Tutsis simply swept the kids up in their arms and carried them away from the advancing Hutu soldiers, then turned them loose in the mountains. There they were roaming the hills, some said, "like packs of wild animals," left to fend for themselves.

This stark reality weighed heavy on me. I brought some others along and we headed to Byumba, the guerrilla army's mountain capital, traveling the mined roads. Our hope was to get permission to open a home for these desperately frightened children.

While I was waiting to meet with a doctor at Byumba, a young child caught my eye. It was a peculiar sight. She was sitting in the back of a dilapidated pickup truck, and her little hands were clinging to a blood-stained blanket. There she was all alone, rocking back and forth on the sun-scorched metal bed of a truck. Her gaze was empty and her little voice weak, but she was softly singing, keeping rhythm as she swayed.

I approached a soldier standing near the truck and asked him, "Who is this little girl?"

"Don't know," he replied.

"Where is she from?"

"Don't know," the soldier said, as he puffed on his cigarette.

I couldn't take my eyes off of her, and pestered the soldier for some answers.

"She's just like all the others—an orphan. Her parents killed. She'll be taken to Rutare," the soldier said.

"What is she singing?" I asked.

"Something in French," he said.

"Do you speak French?" I persisted.

He nodded.

"Do you know what she is singing?"

The soldier reluctantly bent down over his automatic weapon, straining to hear the words. The little girl didn't even notice him. Her gaze was fixed, but she kept rocking back and forth, oblivious to the scorching African sun.

The soldier finally identified the words:

"Jesus . . . loves . . . her . . ." He paused. "No . . . me. Something like that."

"Is she singing 'Jesus loves me this I know, for the Bible tells me so'?" I asked.

He looked up in surprise. "Yes, that's it."

I stared at the sweet little child. The lump in my throat paralyzed my emotions.

This little girl had lost everything. Well, almost everything. I had to conclude that her parents had left her with the most valuable thing they could give her—faith. She knew Jesus loved her and she was clinging to that blood-stained blanket for reassurance. No matter what, Jesus loved her. And I thought of His blood that washes sin away. Heaven knew that much sin had stained the soil of Rwanda, but His blood was sufficient to wash it all away.

That is a picture of the sacrificial gift—the greatest gift of all—the Savior; and we cling to the hope that His shed blood offers to all, His salvation.

I don't know what ever happened to that little girl. She faded into the miserable background with thousands of others just like her, and

I decided right then that with the Lord's help, we would do everything possible to help kids like this little girl.

The rest of the story is that God did enable us to open an orphanage in Kigali, along with the Samaritan Academy where children could receive a Christ-centered education. The next year on December 17, 1995, our team arrived in Kigali for a celebration of joy, bringing shoebox gifts to orphans at our Samaritan Children's Village and to young patients at the Central Hospital of Kigali.

GOD LOVES LITTLE LAMBS, SO DOES MAMA

When my mother heard the story of the little girl, I saw her wheels spinning. She graciously served Operation Christmas Child as honorary chairperson and said, "Franklin, I'd like to have music boxes that play 'Jesus Loves Me' to give these kids."

When Mama had an idea, it was always good and always carried out.

"Consider it done, Mama," I told her.

We found a supplier that could help us and for the first few years, we managed to also supply the lyrics to "Jesus Loves Me" in multiple languages to accompany the music boxes. Some years later, my mother wanted to put the music box inside a stuffed toy—a little lamb. That happened too.

My mother wrote,

> These little lamb music boxes that play "Jesus Loves Me" have a special place in my heart. When Franklin was born, a dear friend of ours gave him a stuffed black lamb that played this song. It was always a comfort to know that our Shepherd cares for His sheep.
>
> I believe one way He does this is through Operation Christmas Child. In every place that Samaritan's Purse distributes shoeboxes, some children are too young or too sick to enjoy a shoebox gift. For these special children, a music box is a perfect gift.
>
> The Bible says we are all lost sheep who need a Shepherd— the Good Shepherd, Jesus Christ. Nowhere is that more evident than when you look into the eyes of a young child—one

of God's little lambs—and find a soul crying out to be loved. After hearing Franklin's story about the little orphan girl in Rwanda, and since I love little lambs, I asked Franklin to find a way to tuck these music boxes inside stuffed toy lambs with a wind up key. They have brought smiles, laughter and comfort to little hearts.

Every story that ever came to our office about the little lambs was copied and sent to my mother until her death, because she loved watching the gentle work of the Shepherd.

IN THE MIDDLE OF THE TABLE SITS "SAM"

We had convened many meetings around a mountain-hewn table discussing how to make Operation Christmas Child known. On the table sat a little musical lamb. Mama had done her part! It was the toy that defined the message of the mission: Jesus Loves Me. That left us staring at the shoebox in the middle of the table—the carrier of the message. Ideas flowed. Some had possibilities, others were just too crazy. One idea that didn't get rejected was, "Let's put wings on the box!"

That rang a bell with me. After all, I was a pilot. We had also depended on air freight to move the shoeboxes from one nation to another. We had the idea drawn up and Todd met with a marketing agency in Uptown Charlotte that had designed the thirty-foot hornet mascot for the Charlotte Hornets basketball team. They examined the box and said, "It will be hard to get wings to stay on a shoebox." But after hearing Todd's presentation and how the project was connected to airplanes, they said, "Leave it with us for a few days and let's see what we can do."

We put in a full day discussing the project in what we call the Bob Pierce room, dedicated in memory of Samaritan's Purse founder Bob Pierce who died of leukemia in 1978. The walls were filled with pictures of the early days of ministry, reminding the entire team of what had been accomplished in the name of the Lord.

Bob had coined a phrase that became a foundational stepping stone for us, "God room." When I first heard that phrase I was twenty-three years old and on a mission trip around the world with Dr. Bob, which I write about in *Rebel with a Cause*. I was exposed to things most people will never see. Everywhere we went the needs were overwhelming and the resources so small (at least that was my assessment). Bob kept talking about "God room" but didn't explain it until I asked.

"Buddy," he said, 'God room' is when you see a need that is bigger than your human abilities to meet it, but you accept the challenge trusting that God will supply the finances, the materials, and the people to meet that need. God room is what's left once we've depleted what we can do. Identify a need, commit it to prayer, have others pray with you, share it with your partners and donors, and then begin to watch God work. You put your trust and faith in Him to do what you cannot do. You allow Him 'room' to work—that's 'God room'."

Days later, we were back at that same conference table staring at this well-constructed prototype—a shoebox with wings. "I like it!" I said. "Let's use it for more than just marketing. This flying shoebox could become our logo—something for children to identify with." We even gave the little guy a name: Sam, short for Samaritan's Purse.

It is a cute little mascot. He's even been used in our printed evangelistic literature and the kids love him. Children who can't read recognize this logo around the world, and hearts swell with excitement when they see it stamped on anything. I have even seen this simple shoebox with airplane wings on it bring tears to children's eyes.

I like to think of the wings as angel wings that carry the Good News of the Gospel right into the hands and hearts of the little children.

I CAN STILL VISUALIZE THE BOX

S even-year-old Alex needed some good news. He had been one of the trembling little lambs, wandering aimlessly in Rwanda.

Alex Nsengimana never knew his father and lost his mother to AIDS when he was four. He and his siblings lived with their grandmother and two uncles. They were tormented by threats from the militia. "Please don't bomb our house," they screamed. The militia complied. Instead, they made the grandmother and one uncle lie on the ground and then tortured them to death as the children watched from a window inside the house. Knowing they would be next, the uncle—who had been spared—told the children to flee to the city where their aunt lived. In time, she put them in an orphanage due to her own illness and died shortly after. Alex tried to understand the whys of his life. If there is a God, why would He let these terrible things happen to his people, his country, his family, himself?

Looking back, Alex began to see that God, for some reason, had protected him because too many incidents had occurred that should have taken his life. At least half a million people had been killed in the span of three months so, the question remained: why was his life spared? This was the perplexing question of his young life—one for which he could find no answer. That is until Operation Christmas Child showed up at his orphanage.

Alex told an audience of three thousand at the OCC Global Connect Conference in Orlando, Florida:

> I had lost all hope. I was standing in the school yard one day with two hundred and fifty other orphans when brightly

colored boxes were given away—one for each orphan. I'll never forget it.

The moment I opened the gift I realized that it was mine. Someone, a stranger I didn't know, had packed it for me and I remember the joy that day. Answers to the question, "Why am I still alive?" started to crystallize when I comprehended that someone did care; I just didn't know the person's name.

To this day, I can visualize that box and some of the things in it: a hair comb, candy cane, and Smarties (the little cellophane wrapped colored candies that I thought were pills—but how could pills look so happy?). If packers could only comprehend what the least little gift means, it would give them a deeper awareness of the value receivers place on these hope-givers. Empty hearts need hope to point them to the Savior.

The orphanage was visited sometime later by the African Children's Choir and I was given the chance to join. I was taken to Uganda to learn English and stories from the Bible. I began cross-referencing verses from the English Bible and the Bible in my own language. I recall finding the passage in Jeremiah 29:11, "I know the plans I have for you," declares the LORD, "plans to prosper you and not to harm you, plans to give you hope and a future" (NIV).

Years later I came to America and Canada with the choir and saw many sites, but nothing made me happier than when I saw the OCC logo. Everywhere I went, there it was! The excitement and memory of the shoebox was rekindled as it had been the seed that planted the Gospel message in my heart. I was able to travel to Minneapolis to see the massive OCC program and learned more about Jesus.

When I accepted Him as my Savior I began to dig deeper—even at age nine—to see how God's plan unfolds. I started to see the terrible war through a different lens, and came to understand that this is why He had spared me—to believe in Him and live for Him the rest of my life so that I could make a difference in others' lives. This is why I had survived the genocide. This has been my great decision in life—to receive eternal life with my Jesus.

Through God's providence and provision, Alex was given the opportunity to attend Bible college in Rochester, Minnesota, and as we finish writing this book (May 2013), he graduated. His desire is to return to Rwanda to plant a church in the same village of his birth, proclaiming God's salvation among his people. "Please pray that I will be faithful to the task and the calling on my life," Alex concluded.

Alex's testimony is the fruit that comes from the seed planted on our side of the shoeboxes. He has said, "What makes the shoebox powerful is the love that prompts each item and the prayer that accompanies the box. If people just pack boxes of toys without believing it can change a kid's life, they are missing the point. And they are missing something greater still—that it can change their lives too!"

So when packers fill boxes, we ask them to pray as they shop, pray as they make selections, pray as they pack, pray as they send, pray as the box is delivered, pray as it is received, and pray as it is used. That's a lot of praying, but the Bible says, "Do everything in the name of the Lord Jesus" (Col. 3:17 HCSB).

GRANDMA PRAYS AS
SHE SHOPS

My father has said, "When I'm asked to list the three most important steps in preparing for an evangelistic mission, my reply is always the same: prayer, prayer, prayer."

God has blessed Operation Christmas Child because of its foundational focus on lifting up the name of Christ. That starts with prayer, lots of it, even for simple things.

This came to mind when we heard a grandmother tell about how prayer impacted her shopping. A preprinted shoebox had been put in her hands one Sunday at church as an incentive to pack it up for OCC.

"I agreed to fill it for a child somewhere in the world. I purchased items, packed the box, and went to bed, but I couldn't sleep for thinking I had bought all the wrong things. Then I remembered Mr. Graham asking that we pray as we pack the box, believing that God would direct each shoebox to a particular child."

This "preyed" on the woman's mind and the next morning she went back to the store with a new mission: to pray for each phase of packing a shoebox. She felt armed this time to make better choices. Grabbing a cart, she headed to the children's department, but was overwhelmed. What size clothing should she buy? What fabric is best for a climate she knows nothing about? What would make the child happy? Then it hit her that she was getting the "cart before the horse." She realized she was still trying to fill a box for a child she didn't know—but God knew.

She stopped in the aisle and silently prayed, "Lord you know what a child's need is and which child will receive this box. I cannot possibly know such things, but You do. Direct me in making choices that will bless this little one in ways I cannot imagine, because most of all, this gift is a means to demonstrate Your love. Please help me."

"When I looked up, clerks wondered if I was okay. Now I was, prayed up and depending on the Lord to help me every step of the way. 'Can I assist you?' a saleslady asked."

She told the woman about her exciting challenge—to shop for a child she's never met, who lives in a part of the world where she's never been. The sales lady said, "Oh! That sounds like an Operation Christmas Child challenge." The grandmother smiled and whispered, "Thank you, Lord."

The ladies began making selections and then Grandma headed to the toy department. She had her eye on a particular doll, but when she picked it up, she knew it would never fit inside the box she had at home. Making her way to the shoe department while praying, with doll in hand, a salesman smiled. "We don't sell doll shoes, but how can I help?"

"Oh, I'm trying to find a box to hold this doll and some other items," she explained. The clerk said, "A shoebox for a doll? Is this for Operation Christmas Child?" She smiled and said, "You understand?"

"Oh yes," he said. "We have people in here all the time, but they usually have a flying shoebox on their shirts or jackets." Worried, she explained that she didn't have room for shoes and a doll, but she badly wanted a boot box. Another shopper nearby overheard, reached in her bag and pulled a pair of boots from the box, and handed Grandma the boot box. "Use this one. God bless you for what you are doing," the stranger said.

Grandma struggled between whether to cry or laugh, but she settled for hugging the lady and returning the blessing by sharing how the Lord had led her back to the store to "pray a shoebox" together. What a testimony this was to everyone involved.

A "Round Table"
in God Room

R wanda was certainly the topic of conversation around the table as we discussed the disastrous distribution, countered by the evidence that shoebox gifts were making a big difference in packer's hearts and little hearts who would receive them.

With everything Samaritan's Purse was doing around the world, I felt it was important to assemble a base team in Boone that represented every facet of Operation Christmas Child. In January 1995, we spent a great deal of time discussing "how to give away gifts to children." God guided and directed in each detail, bringing resolution to the "what ifs," by dealing with the "why nots?"

Why not organize the distributions by controlling the numbers? Why not choose the locations? Why not mobilize local volunteers to "come and help us"? Out of that came so many important components that stabilized the process.

This is where we began to see how evangelism could become not only the focus of the shoebox gifts, but the centerpiece of the distributions themselves. The team began developing programs for the children that would come ahead of the gift giving. There could be puppet shows, skits, and singing all focused on telling the greatest story of all.

We began to recruit pastors and church leaders who could organize such programs in advance to present the Gospel to the children in their own language, giving the pastor the premier opportunity to share the Christmas story with the children. This brought spiritual purpose to the distributions and anchored the enthusiasm. We knew we didn't want to crush the children's joy, but we also knew that we had to be in control of the emotional reaction to "gift-receiving."

Gathered around the table we also wondered how we could get vendors to supply their products for the boxes. We looked at Sam sitting on the table and discussed filling twenty winged boxes with items we hoped to receive—things like Life Savers and Beanie Babies. If we customized such a box for each vendor, with just their product alone, and sent it to them, maybe they would help us. Our round-table discussion (around a rectangle table) eventually led us to send twenty presentation boxes to a variety of vendors.

We had learned through inspecting the boxes that when we had to remove certain items like food and liquids that may spoil and spill, we had to replace them with other things for the boxes to be adequately filled. We had made similar requests when Samaritan's Purse needed blankets and other items by the thousands, and we have always appreciated corporations that would donate such things, known as gift-in-kind (a form of charitable giving through the donation of products and services in lieu of monetary donations).

The presentations, however, were not received well. We had hoped that the shoeboxes with wings would bring enthusiastic responses, but most corporations informed us that their charitable resources were already committed. The fruitless effort reminded us again that if the program was going to be successful, the Lord would work in the hearts of the people to respond.

In years to come, He did just that. Women's groups began knitting clubs, donating booties, blankets and sweaters. Teenage girls held jewelry-making parties. Children canvassed small-town businesses to contribute a variety of items that fit perfectly into shoeboxes.

We learned that the key to every aspect of OCC was with individuals. This was made evident when Dr. Melvin Cheatham introduced me to Jim Hodges, owner of the Royal Paper Box Company in California. Jim loved OCC and when he noticed the variance in shoebox sizes he offered to make boxes that would identify them as OCC boxes. While it was not possible to use the boxes in every situation, it did become a great incentive for people who requested them.

We turned our focus to the most significant component: mobilizing Christians to get involved. Getting the Gospel out was the objective, and the body of Christ has made that happen.

Taking Charge

With more ministry opportunities developing, Todd transitioned from director of the project to handling the legal aspects of trade marking the name Operation Christmas Child as well as the logo. He continued working with corporate sponsors, and dealt with the varied tax issues of non-profit work domestically and the duty tax internationally.

We had been looking for someone to step into the role Todd had filled and the name that kept popping up was Jim Harrelson. Jim and his wife Grace had served in Sudan with African Inland Mission (AIM). Jim had gained a great deal of international field experience and felt the Lord might be leading him to join Samaritan's Purse. In 1993, he and Grace agreed to serve with us and Jim became our project director for Somalia. In fact, he was our man on the ground when things erupted there. The Battle of Mogadishu (also referred to as Black Hawk Down) necessitated us having to leave the country. The Lord used Jim to safely evacuate our team.

Joining the staff in Boone, Jim began working with Kenney Isaacs on several projects in 1994 including Rwanda and joined Todd's team later that year as preparations were made for OCC distributions.

When 1995 rolled around, I asked Jim Harrelson to take charge of OCC and bring it to the next level. Jim was excited. He couldn't have been given a more compelling assignment: to develop every aspect of OCC to carry the Gospel to the ends of the earth.

Jim has a real heart for children, and he and Grace were both excited to think that OCC's future was in child evangelism. There are not many ministries that focus on this in remote parts of the world and Jim wasted no time in getting started.

By 1997, OCC had grown significantly and it was time to make it a department of its own, while remaining a project of Samaritan's Purse. The Lord had prepared Jim for this task. With a small team of Randy Riddle, Sheila Storie, and Travis Critcher, the Lord was stretching OCC in significant ways. Twenty years later, Jim is at the helm as vice president of OCC, a project with a strong and complex, yet well executed, infrastructure. He has developed a committed staff that oversees the logistics and ministry aspects of this massive undertaking.

Another important step for us was relocating our processing center from Huntsville to Charlotte. We also established a processing center in Boone by expanding our World Medical Mission warehouse and allocating space for OCC. The decision proved to be a boost for the program. Kenney and Jim also began recruiting volunteers for these locations (not an easy task). But remembering the "God room" principle, we did what we could and asked the Lord to bless with His provision. After all, it is by the work of the Holy Spirit that people's hearts are touched to serve Him. And they came, by the thousands.

BOXES WINGING THEIR WAY

G ood logistical support is imperative to ministry, but the
most important to me was the evangelism component. We
began exploring Bible-based literature that could be provided to
the recipients of the shoebox gifts. This led to partnerships with
Christian organizations that had already developed evangelism
materials for children.

The Lord worked through Jim to build a fortified team and they
learned all they could with the hope that one day we would have the
resources, the know-how, the people, and funding to produce our
own materials. Our aim was to teach children about Jesus, the Bible,
and prayer—the keys to bringing lost sheep to the Savior. The pages
ahead document so well just how this has been accomplished and
blessed by God.

This is what compelled me to write *Miracle in a Shoebox* and,
some years later, another children's book entitled *A Wing and a
Prayer*, as a way of explaining salvation and the importance of developing a relationship with God through prayer. It wasn't long before
we began to hear from those who stood with us in this endeavor, and
God used it to encourage us. A donor wrote:

> Dear Friends in Christ, what a joy to be involved with
> Operation Christmas Child. Seventy colorful boxes went
> winging their way to Boone—the first leg of the long jour-
> ney—but oh the party we had at church, packing and wrap-
> ping these boxes. From small children to grandparents, we
> all had a ball!

Tears and prayers went winging their way heavenward, too, asking the Lord to guide the boxes, matching the contents with just the right children. We agonized over each gift that went into the boxes, dreaming of the little hands that would open them. Before sending the gifts on their way, we gathered and prayed for each worker, each prayer, every volunteer, every donor, every staff member and all the partners along the path of delivery.

We know the prayers will be heard and answered, as they wing their way into little hearts and treasured souls.

VOLUNTEER VALUE

Thanksgiving 1995 arrived and we had staffed the processing center in Boone to work continuously through the holiday weekend, but we never expected to witness an outpouring of enthusiastic volunteers. They came from all over mountain counties surrounding Boone and states as far away as Oklahoma. We had families arrive in campers and motor homes, asking if they could "plug in" somewhere on the property.

Moms, dads, teens, and children also plugged in along the processing lines, retiring at night to their quarters on wheels. There were no complaints or needs, just others serving to make Operation Christmas Child a success that year. And it was—more than we could have ever thought possible—"God room."

The same thing was happening in Calgary, Alberta, where our Canadian office is based. Our processing centers are nerve centers, because God's people are there, connecting a resource to a need—children who have nothing. The Gospel message would soon be on its way to Eastern Europe, Africa, the Middle East, and Central and South America.

Collection centers were organized in key regions of the sending countries and relay stations were being established by people who were anxious to participate. Excitement brewed as people heard about OCC through churches. Others came to help us after hearing about it on television and through public service announcements (PSA) on radio.

It was through a PSA that Lynnette Dallmann from Allentown, Pennsylvania, came to help. She had been asking the Lord where she could serve Him. Being persuaded by a friend, she became a volunteer and is now with us as a regional coordinator. "I can't imagine life without OCC," she told us. Just as God so often directs, her husband, who works in radio, now serves as an OCC media coordinator. You guessed it—he oversees the placement of PSAs. When God calls, He equips, and if we look close enough, we see that His work is full circle, completing what He starts.

Among a Mountain
of Shoeboxes

In Germany, this is exactly what happened. Thorsten Behnke, not a Christian at first, heard about Operation Christmas Child and some controversy about the evangelism component of the project. It raised his curiosity and he decided to learn more. When he did, he became excited about what OCC was doing for children. He contacted OCC asking how he could help and was given a copy of my book *Rebel with a Cause*. He began a serious journey to find out if there really was a God after all.

In the meantime, Thorsten wanted to help us find warehouse space. In the process he was invited to visit an evangelical church. The pastor encouraged him to attend services which put him in touch with Christians, and the preaching of God's Word began to take root.

By himself in the warehouse one evening finishing his work, he had a strong awareness of God's presence and knew he was not alone. There, in the midst of a mountain of shoeboxes, Thorsten responded to the Holy Spirit's call to settle his account with Jesus Christ. In obedience, he repented of sin and received salvation, committing his life wholly to Him.

Thorsten still serves OCC, helping to mobilize others to "come and help us." As a taxi driver, he never fails to share his testimony with those who ride in his cab, many who inquire why he has a Bible in the seat rack, along with a supply of OCC literature.

Taking a ride in this cab often leads others to a future destination that is certain—the hope of Heaven.

THE CHURCH IS KEY

The church is the key to collecting shoeboxes and the key to distributing them. While Operation Christmas Child administers the massive task of collecting the shoeboxes and arranging transport, ninety-nine percent of the boxes are distributed by our ministry partners around the world. The gifts are put into the hands of Christians living in these countries: people who speak the language and have hearts to be the light of God's love. Putting these shoebox gifts into their hands raises the presence of the church on both sides of the box—the sending and the receiving—and others looking on see the church reaching out to people in Jesus' name. Having the churches involved also establishes a solid base of prayer support. This is vital to doing God's work, "for the equipping of the saints for the work of the ministry, for the edifying of the body of Christ, till we all come to the unity of the faith and of the knowledge of the Son of God" (Eph. 4:12–13).

We were thankful for the ministry base already in place. Samaritan's Purse had worked in many countries and we always worked through the church. Likewise, the Billy Graham Evangelistic Association (BGEΛ) had done the same in preparation for crusades for over forty years. This gave OCC a firm foundation on which to build a network of pastors, churches, and Christian workers who would partner with us in getting the shoeboxes to the children.

Our team has worked hard to identify church pastors and leaders in countries we go to. While we don't always do shoebox distributions in churches, we work with them to identify other venues so that the church can be lifted up in the eyes of the people.

We also work with parachurch organizations like Bible societies and evangelical mission organizations—the community of believers that make up the body of Christ. They take the responsibility of mobilizing and training others to serve Christ through OCC. This is essential in doing effective ministry; working with one another in the name of Jesus.

Church planting has been one of the great surprises and blessings of this program; we never dreamed in 1993 that a simple shoebox would be used in God's hands to add to His church. "[God] is able to do immeasurably more than all we ask or imagine, according to His power that is at work within us" (Eph. 3:20 NIV).

God has used the simple shoebox to open up hearts to His salvation. It spurs new believers on in the faith and establishes Bible-believing churches in some of the most unlikely places around the globe, as seen within the pages of this book. We give Him the praise and glory, for Jesus said, "I will build My church" (Matt. 16:18 HCSB).

SHOEBOX SUNDAY

Good works through His church made up of His servants, and Operation Christmas Child depends on the support of the churches to do this work. And we haven't been disappointed.

Two very close friends of mine—senior pastors of large churches—invited me to preach between Thanksgiving and Christmas in 1995. They had gotten on board with us from the earliest days of Operation Christmas Child. "Come out and preach for us and you'll have a chance to see how excited our people are about OCC," they both said.

Their congregations had been packing and collecting shoeboxes. It sounded like a good idea, so I flew to Albuquerque, New Mexico, and preached on Sunday morning for Skip Heitzig at Calvary Chapel. That afternoon I traveled to Riverside, California, to preach for Greg Laurie at Harvest Christian Fellowship.

Greg and Skip had their own struggles growing up and I think it tenderized their hearts for what kids deal with. Greg's mother was a beautiful woman who married seven times. Greg was bounced around from father to father and dabbled in drugs; but while in high school he heard a street evangelist and was saved.

Skip had wandered into the world of physic power, but one day the Lord got hold of his heart. He was watching television one night and saw my father preaching at one of his crusades. Skip went to the refrigerator to get a beer figuring he would find a better channel once he sat down, but by the time he got back in front of the TV, he heard my father giving the invitation. Skip listened and thought, *Man—glad I'm not there. I'd be walking down the aisle like all those other people.* About the time he finished the thought, my father said, "For those of you watching by television—you need to come to Christ." Skip put his beer down, repented of his sin, and was saved.

These two pastors really got into OCC, and so did their congregations. They stacked boxes up in their church sanctuaries. There were many hundreds the first year and, each year after, many thousands. Other churches began hearing about it and began doing the same. It came to be known as "Shoebox Sunday," and churches often schedule it following National Collection Week, the third week of November.

We could not do OCC without the churches; in fact, I wouldn't do it without the churches. Why? Because boxes come into the church with prayer and go out of the church with prayer. Church members pack their boxes as they pray. We get boxes from others, but we want the church backing this remarkable opportunity for the Gospel. Without prayer power, the boxes will simply be gifts enjoyed for a few days and then forgotten. But the Gospel does not return void—it is God's Word.

I can remember preaching for Skip Heitzig on this special day. He invited the kids to gather around the boxes and have a special time of prayer, asking the Lord to guide them to the right children so that the Gospel message will be understood. We have no idea where these boxes will end up, but God does, and we've watched Him direct many of them to children with very specific needs that are met by what is in the shoebox. The only way it can be explained is God.

After the service, a young woman approached me with tears in her eyes, carrying a shoebox she had carefully packed and said, "I remember seeing you in the refugee camp in Bosnia. We lived in tents and could only bathe once every few weeks. In the cold winters there was no heat and everything smelled stale. Then the shoeboxes came." She told me how she had received a box one year and everything was bright and clean. She remembered getting a doll and a scarf and hat. She embraced the box she was holding as though she was back in the moment. Then she said, "Mr. Graham, could you take this box to a young girl like I was when I got mine?"

I was amazed to look at this young woman who had come to know Christ. She was now living in America, working at Walmart and attending the University of New Mexico. Does prayer for a simple shoebox given to a child work? You bet it does!

WILL YOU GO TO SARAJEVO?

Wrapping up National Collection Week and "Shoebox Sunday" dedications in November 1995, plans were being nailed down for press conferences, and distribution teams were being organized to head out immediately after the press events in December. Russian Antonov 124 cargo planes carried gifts from Charlotte, Calgary, and Long Beach to Stansted, England, creating quite a buzz at each of the press conferences. These mighty planes had once been used to transport weaponry; now they were loaded with shoeboxes that would take the Gospel to many nations. What the Lord had done in two short years was nothing but "God room" on full display.

Because I had been unable to lead a distribution team the first two years of the project, I wasn't about to miss the chance this time around. I called a number of people and asked, "Will you go with me to Sarajevo?" Mary Damron responded, "Okay Brother Graham, just tell me when." My friend Dennis Agajanian, a Christian recording artist said, "See ya there" (if you've ever seen Dennis you would know that I brought him along for protection). Dr. Melvin Cheatham and his wife Sylvia, who had traveled with me to some of the hot spots of the world and performed surgery on victims of war, always kept their bags packed and ready.

Then I called my friends and recording artists Ricky Skaggs and his wife Sharon White and invited them to join me. They're not afraid of anything because they go in the strength of the Lord. Tommy Coomes and Al Denson also agreed to come. Kenney had assembled some folks to join us for logistical support and I told them, "Meet me in Stansted, England."

With deadlines, commitments, end-of-year business and board meetings—not to mention Christmas preparation with the family—I didn't need one more thing to do. But when I got a call from Mary Damron, my schedule abruptly changed.

FROM WEST VIRGINIA HOLLERS
TO PENNSYLVANIA AVENUE ✳

M ary had been busy all year collecting more shoeboxes for God. She went from twelve hundred in 1994 to collecting over six thousand the next year (I guess she was trying to stack a mountain of shoeboxes as high as the West Virginia hills). She had traveled all over the state, and had even gone to other states representing Operation Christmas Child. She had become a bit of a local celebrity and was written up in a local West Virginia newspaper. Who would ever think that a White House staffer would get hold of a small article from the hills?

President Bill Clinton was planning to send troops to Bosnia to solidify the implementation of the Dayton Peace Accord, scheduled to be signed in France the day after his upcoming news conference. He wanted to showcase several volunteer civilians who had already been involved in Bosnia. They scanned the Internet and stumbled across the write-up about Mary. She was a perfect fit.

In early December, Mary answered the phone at her home and got the shock of her life.

"Is this Mary Damron?" the caller said.

"Yep," Mary answered.

"This is the White House."

"No it ain't."

"Yes, it is." There was a long pause. "I'm calling on behalf of the President."

"No you ain't."

Mary couldn't believe that the White House would call her. Once she realized that somebody was really calling on behalf of the President, she took down the information and then called me.

"Brother Graham," she said, "the Prez-i-dent wants me up there in Washington."

"That's wonderful, Mary!" I replied.

"I don't feel comfortable going up there."

"Well, Mary," I said, "that doesn't matter. He's the President, and if he calls you to the White House, you should go."

There was a long pause. "How 'bout if you go with me?" she asked.

"Mary, the President hasn't invited me," I protested.

"If you can't go, I ain't goin'." Mary said.

I knew that Mary could not decline such an invitation, and I agreed to call the White House and try to get it all worked out.

When I called the President's social liaison and explained Mary's hesitation to come without me, the lady politely said, "But, Mr. Graham, the President hasn't invited you."

"I realize that," I said, "but Mary is uneasy about coming. She'll feel much better if I come with her."

"You wouldn't be able to attend the sessions," the aide asserted. "You'd have to sit out in the hall."

"That won't bother me," I said. "I spent half my school years sitting in the hall."

The White House agreed that I could accompany Mary and her family. I flew to Bluefield, West Virginia, the nearest airport to Ikes Fork, to meet Mary, her husband, and two of her three children, then headed to Dulles Airport. I had requested a van to meet us upon arrival and take us into the heart of the city. When we touched down and unloaded the luggage, a stretch limousine pulled up alongside the plane. I tried to explain to the driver that a mistake had been made. "We are supposed to have a van take us into D.C.," I insisted.

"Mr. Graham," the driver said, "all we have available right now are limos, but we'll only charge you the van rate."

It wasn't the cost I was concerned about as much as it was the image. The driver convinced me that if we were going to get downtown on time, we'd have to take the limousine, so all five of us piled into the polished black stretch limo. Mary's two children thought they had died and gone to Heaven.

"Mama!" her teenage daughter, Ashley, exclaimed. "They got a bar! In a car!"

"Don't touch that," Mary whispered, pushing the little girl's hand away.

"And peanuts!" her son added.

"Don't eat those," Mary scolded.

But they just couldn't resist. They pushed every button they could find, ignoring their mother's chiding and the monuments and historical buildings along the way. I got a kick out of watching their eyes snap. I am sure the driver had to wonder who had come to town.

"You know, Mama," Mary's son said with a slow drawl as he fiddled with the backseat control panel, "You saw Brother Graham on the TV, went out and got some shoeboxes, took 'em down thar to Carolina, you got sent off to Boze-ne-a, and now the Prez-i-dent's done called you to Washin'ton. You're nothin' but a Mama Gump."

With that, I lost it. I couldn't help but laugh—and so did Mary. He was referring, of course, to the novel and movie *Forrest Gump*, in which a country boy (portrayed in the movie by Tom Hanks) from Greenbow, Alabama, stumbles onto one momentous thing after another throughout life and ends up meeting the President.

From the Poor House
to the White House

After a rather entertaining ride into D.C., we arrived at the hotel in time to meet with representatives from the White House. They were coming to introduce themselves to Mary and to double-check her story so that the President could be fully and accurately briefed. By the end of the interview, Mary had disarmed them, and they left that night quite impressed by a little mountain woman from West Virginia.

The next morning the Damron family emerged from their rooms wearing the new sweatshirts I had given them that had the logo and Operation Christmas Child embroidered into the fabric. On the way to the White House Mary asked me, "Brother Graham, I've been wonderin'—do you think I should pray fer the Prez-i-dent? Do you think he'd mind if I prayed fer him in that there Oval Office?"

I was touched by her sensitivity. At the same time I was amazed by her boldness. "No, Mary, I don't think he'd mind," I said.

We arrived at the Guard Gate off Pennsylvania Avenue and after receiving clearance from security, we were ushered into the White House. Following the news conference, Mary's family and I were ushered into the Oval Office for pictures. When I walked through the door and spotted Mary, I noticed that she was stooped over her blue canvas travel bag she had been holding.

I thought, *Oh boy, what has she got in there?*

"Mr. Prez-i-dent," she raised up, "I got somethin' fer you."

My heart melted when she pulled out one of the empty shoe-boxes that had been specially printed for OCC.

"Mr. Prez-i-dent, will you fill this one fer me?"

The President seemed truly surprised by Mary's modest request. "Mary," he said, "I'll be glad to fill a shoebox for you."

When the President stretched out his hands to receive the box, Mary, as bold as a lion and as gentle as a dove, said, "Mr. Prez-i-dent, do you *car* if I pray fer you?"

In that fleeting moment, the President became solemn. A little mountain woman took him completely off guard, but he graciously agreed. "I would appreciate that, Mary. Thank you."

Mary took the lead in joining our hands and then prayed a short prayer. When I opened my eyes, the President seemed moved. Maybe he could sense that this woman's power within was God's strength from above. There's no question that day in the Oval Office; Mary made a lasting impression with the commander-in-chief. After all, our brief photo session with the President of the United States turned into a twenty-five-minute chat instead, ending with a little prayer meeting with the King of kings. In one twenty-four-hour period, God brought Mary from the poor house to the White House.

The Bible says, "Not many of you were wise by human standards; not many were influential; not many were of noble birth. But God chose the foolish things of the world to shame the wise; God chose the weak things of the world to shame the strong. He chose the lowly things of this world and the despised things—and the things that are not—to nullify the things that are, so that no one may boast before him" (1 Cor. 1:26–29 NIV).

A few days later, our team would leave for Bosnia armed with Mary Damron and a special shoebox packed by the First Family. "Mary," I told her, "we'll find an extraordinary child to receive the President's shoebox."

The Chatter of the Press, the Buzz of the Planes

B efore beginning that search, we had press conferences to attend. Many staff, corporate sponsors, volunteers, and school children gathered in airports around the United States, Canada, and England for regional shoebox send-offs. The first of these events took place at the Long Beach Airport in California.

Russ Busby, my father's longtime photographer who lived in southern California came to document the event and brought with him Louis Zamperini, a former American Olympic long-distance runner and World War II POW. He had been saved at my father's 1949 Los Angeles crusade and came to lend his support to the event. Greg Laurie, senior pastor of Harvest Christian Fellowship in Riverside, California, addressed the crowd. He turned and pointed to the gift-filled Antonov looming behind him and said, "Instead of being an instrument of war, this airplane is being used as an instrument of peace, an instrument for bringing a little light into a very dark place."

Amid the deafening roar of engines, onlookers watched as the Antonov took off—on a mission of love.

The event had everybody talking—even the media. CNN reported, "The holidays will be brighter for the children of Bosnia . . ." CBS Evening News ran a story, "More than 800,000 Christmas shoeboxes donated for children in Bosnia, Croatia, Rwanda, and Russia." The Associated Press sent over the wire that "Volunteers from Samaritan's Purse Christian relief agency ship the shoeboxes to children . . . collected from all over the country, from the White House to the hills of Appalachia." *The Los Angeles Times* printed, "School children watched workers load about 70,000 shoeboxes . . . onto a cargo plane headed for war-torn [countries]." *USA Today* wrote that 800,000 shoeboxes had been collected "by more than 2,000 churches in the USA and Canada."

Excitement had everyone stirred up and we hadn't even started the trip.

THE BIG SEND-OFF

Stansted Airport is thirty miles northeast of London. The airfield had been used during the Second World War by the Royal Air Force and the US Army Air Corps as a bomber airfield and maintenance depot. We had been working closely with Graeme Pearce of HeavyLift Cargo Group, the giant worldwide freight carrier that had among its fleet these Russian cargo planes known as "The Big Muscle," because of their capacity to transport almost anything. HeavyLift had been a key partner in transporting shoeboxes. The big "H" could easily be seen on the nose of these massive machines that took to the sky. Graeme was captivated by the shoebox program and personally traveled with us on several distribution trips. It seemed fitting to hold our first international press conference at this location.

December 16, 1995 was a cold, dreary, Saturday. In spite of the threat of snow, media outlets were there to cover the event. Mounting the platform I looked into a gathering crowd of bundled people from head to toe, leaving only enough uncovered to see and breathe. But it didn't cramp the enthusiasm. For the first time in history, five giant Russian Antonov 124s were sitting on the same ramp at the same time. With a wing span of over two hundred and seventy feet from tip to tip (nearly the length of a football field), it was a grand event for Operation Christmas Child's first international send-off.

It was an amazing moment for the Gospel. Addressing those present I said, "This project is about giving to children—children who have been devastated by war and famine. We are going with these planes to share the love shown by people all over the world, and to tell children that there is hope in God."

By 10:00 a.m., the five planes started their engines and began their historic journey: one bound for Africa, another headed for the Middle East, and three winging their way to Croatia. Children all over the world had no idea that they were about to experience Christmas for the very first time.

Jim Harrelson boarded one of the Antonovs with Ross Robinson from Prestonwood Baptist Church in Dallas, Texas (now with OCC), and retired US Air Force General Tom Sadler, an enthusiastic support of OCC. The crew invited them to sit in the cockpit and the guys were excited about having a bird's-eye view right into Zagreb.

All three planes bound for Croatia left Stansted in snow and things didn't improve much from there. Visibility was nearly zero as we approached Zagreb airport in Croatia. These planes had been required to make an instrument approach due to the weather. The Antonov carrying Jim Harrelson and team were praying hard as they watched the shaping of a perilous landing. Their pilot intercepted the localizer inside the outer marker, which did not allow him enough time to stabilize his approach. Keep in mind these are huge aircraft. When the pilot broke out of the clouds, his craft was not lined up on the center of the runway but off to the left side. He had already pulled the power back and the plane began to settle half on the runway and half off in soft mud. To avoid a catastrophe, the pilot gave it full power. This huge aircraft shook and trembled and its massive engines tried to get the plane airborne again. Miraculously, the huge airplane was able to suck itself up out of the mud and the pilot flew the next approach and came back for the second attempt and brought the plane in for a safe, but nail-biting, landing. General Sadler said to Jim as they deplaned, "After multiple missions in Korea and Vietnam, that's the closest to death I have ever come!"

When the rest of us on the other planes realized what had happened, it was not just a close call—it was a miracle! Had the plane crashed, the loss of lives would have been catastrophic. The Lord obviously had plans for these men and for Operation Christmas Child.

NASHVILLE PLAYS WELL IN THE BIHAC POCKET

The weather continued to challenge our movements in the region but we stayed busy doing distributions in and around Zagreb, including a school gymnasium in the Bihac Pocket. Surrounded by enemy forces it was a very dangerous place, and getting a group in there safely was of paramount importance.

Bihac had been in the news. The enemy had surrounded the area for three years, and Bihac had endured daily assaults by mortar shells. It's still hard to fathom that anyone could have survived the constant bombardment. Those who did, suffered severe injuries.

Determined to do a distribution in a large bombed out sports arena, we recognized the event could easily turn into a riot from the children's enthusiasm alone. But we managed to keep the activities tightly controlled.

The music helped. In fact, it was a hit with the kids. Ricky and Sharon sang for an excited crowd of almost three thousand children. Most of them had known only the terrifying sights and sounds of war during their young lives. Many had lost family members—often a parent—in the conflict.

For many, it was the first time their terrorized hearts were happy. One of the most touching moments, especially for Mary, was when we found that extraordinary child to receive the President's shoebox. I had noticed a seven-year-old girl named Zlada. Her china doll face was framed with brown hair cut in page-boy style. She was wrapped up in a tan coat with a fuzzy collar, easy to cuddle. Through an interpreter, her mother told us the story.

"It was peaceful and quiet," Zlada's mother said. "My daughter had gone outside to play with the other kids on their sleds. "Because it was Orthodox Christmas, we thought there would be no shelling that day. We were wrong. With no warning, shrapnel hit Zlada in the left knee. Doctors had to amputate her leg and for two and a half years, she walked and played on crutches. Nothing could stop her. She was brave."

When I took Zlada on stage to meet Mary, the place erupted because to the town folks of Bihac, she was the image of bravery.

There was a tender moment on the platform as Mary hugged the girl and told about meeting the President of the United States, asking him to fill an empty shoebox for a special child. Mary handed that same box to Zlada to empty; her little face glowed with thanks.

We ended the program with the familiar Christmas carol, "Silent Night." Throughout the crowd, young Bosnian girls and boys could be seen mouthing the words in English. These children had come to receive boxes filled with love. But they received something more— the opportunity to hear the Gospel message in word and song.

Watching Mary relate to children was a real lesson for me. We had visited a hospital ward in Bihac and I came across a very sick little boy. I placed a box next to him, but he showed no response. I opened the package and tipped it slightly so he could see what was inside. He wouldn't even smile. I tried to get him to play with one of the cars, but he just wasn't interested.

I started looking around for some support. One of the nurses explained that months before, the little boy had witnessed the murder of his parents and hadn't responded to anyone since that day. I'm sure the nurse thought I was offended that the boy didn't show any interest, but that wasn't the case; my heart broke for him. I just couldn't walk away without making some kind of connection.

TROUBADOURS OF GOOD WILL
AND THE HILLBILLY ANGEL

I spotted Mary playing with a group of kids. Ricky, Sharon, and Dennis were like troubadours of goodwill, roaming from ward to ward playing their guitars as the children watched and listened with delight. I hollered above the music, "Mary! I've got a special child for you."

With one big sweep, Mary hugged the group of little ones she had been playing with and was over to the bed railing in a flash. "Mary," I said, "he just needs a little love."

Gently pushing me aside, Mary leaned over the metal bar and started unpacking the box of toys, but the boy's expression didn't change. Mary began lightly poking him in the ribs and making funny faces. She took the little toy car and followed a make-believe road across his legs and arms, imitating the sounds of a rattling engine and screeching brakes. I stood over Mary's shoulder and watched the little boy's eyes follow her hands. Mary kept on until a feeble smile slipped across the mouth of his sad little face. Mary had broken through.

Within minutes the boy had dumped the contents of the box in his lap. For the first time, the hospital staff heard him giggling with delight as they gathered around to see the amazing transformation. Mary and the boy were both talking a mile a minute—he in Croatian and Mary in hillbilly English. Neither one of them had a clue what the other was saying, but there they were, Mary's eyes reflecting the twinkle in his, as they bantered back and forth, communicating through the universal language of love.

Mary always made eye contact with the children and made a point to treat each child the same—special. Mary was not offended by their dirty bodies and dreadful smell. Her affection, in many cases, was the only medicine these little ones needed, which proved, "A merry heart does good, like medicine" (Prov. 17:22).

"Mary," I asked her later, "how is it that you have so much compassion and love for these children?"

She said, "Brother Franklin, I see myself in these people. Like them, I growed up hard; had a tough childhood. We didn't have money. We stayed hungry. In the wintertime we couldn't keep warm. I know what they're goin' through."

I began to see some similarities between the hollers of West Virginia and the mountains of Croatia and Bosnia.

People often make excuses about why God can't use them: "I can't speak their language—they won't understand me." "Their skin is a different color than mine—they won't accept me." "How can I relate to their problems?"

But like the apostle Paul, Mary knew "Whether well fed or hungry, whether living in plenty or in want. I can do everything through [Christ] who gives me strength" (Phil. 4:12–13 NIV).

Mary couldn't speak the language of the Bosnian people but she found a way to "love on them a little bit." That, they understood. As the British would say, she was willing to "give it a go." A simple country girl found a way to present a simple shoebox gift and demonstrate the simple, but profound message of God's love. Within two weeks, God had demonstrated His power in Mary to speak with boldness to the President, and to speak in tenderness to the least of these.

CROSSING MOUNT IGMAN
TO SNIPER ALLEY

The weather was frigid—foggy, drizzly, and damp. The team carefully selected to go into Sarajevo had turned in for a good night's sleep. I met with Kenney and said, "I'm going to cancel the trip to Sarajevo. It's too dangerous. It would be different if it was just you and me, but I'm responsible for all of these people."

"But Franklin, we've committed to do this." Kenney was stunned. I knew the tremendous amount of work that had gone into planning for Sarajevo. Kenney had met with the Minister of Education in Sarajevo to get clearance for our travel and the actual distribution, including a musical concert with Ricky Skaggs. This had not been an easy task. He had even sought assistance from UNPROFOR (the United Nations Protection Force) for Bosnia and Croatia, who had agreed to provide armed escorts from the end of Croatian territory into Bosnia. Armed vehicles had been scheduled to accompany our convoy, providing security front and back. This had been a huge answer to prayer; so I understood why Kenney's face fell when I told him we shouldn't go.

Kenney is capable and talented. He is also a good soldier. He left my room and handwrote a letter that night and faxed it to Sarajevo. "We're cancelling the trip and we will find a way to send the gifts for the children another way." When that was done, he also cancelled the convoy that had carefully been worked out.

The next day as everyone stayed busy with distributions, many of the team members asked, "What time do we leave for Sarajevo? We're sure looking forward to what is in store." We had even invited a representative, Barbara James, from Thomas Nelson Publishers (who later joined the OCC staff in Boone). I had just released two books with them and they had partnered with Samaritan's Purse in marketing the books in order to gain support for Operation Christmas Child. They were thrilled to be invited on this historic distribution inside Sarajevo.

I began to question my decision. After all, I had asked these very people weeks before if they were willing to risk a trip into Sarajevo; not one of them hesitated.

THE MOST DANGEROUS ROAD
IN THE WORLD

✳

K enney, we have to go to Sarajevo," I said with resolve. They're prayed up. They're ready. I can't tell them no!"

Kenney looked perplexed, conflicted, but ready to go! He has worked with me a long time. He understands the decision-making process. He is cut out for last-minute changes and doesn't get ruffled. But his wheels were turning. "I don't think we'll get UNPROFOR to reinstate the escort; they are angry." Kenney was right. They would not even consider the idea and it left us with only one option: drive across Mount Igman at our own risk which, at the time, was the most dangerous road in the world. Just the week before, members of the American Embassy had been killed when their car slid off the road and tumbled down the mountain.

My experiences have taught me that working overseas, while rewarding and fulfilling, is not always safe. I have dodged bullets in Lebanon, navigated minefields in Angola, witnessed the aftermath of genocide in Rwanda, and been in many other hot spots of the world. But even in danger, I never questioned if I should be there. Peace was present because there was no doubt that God had called me to this work. The staff feels the same. When God's Spirit prods our spirits, we go. Often it leads us right into the ditches and gutters that litter our world. We have to slip into spiritual armor to serve the King of kings and Lord of lords.

The best vehicles were no longer available. Kenney found two small vans and had chains put on the front wheels, hoping it would pull the vehicles adequately through the heavy snow that covered the pass.

I gathered our small team for a time of prayer, asking for God's protection and guidance every mile of the way. Two feet of snow blanketed the ground with more coming down. The road was narrow, making it difficult to pass the oncoming traffic pouring out of Bosnia. The mountain pass—a dirt road steep and narrow—wound through the forest and was the only landline in and out of Sarajevo.

Kenney led the way, but we had to work our way around the trucks while trying to keep our caravan together. One of our vehicles, however, ended up in the ditch to avoid hitting an oncoming truck. There was not much more than sand between the two vehicles because at times the road narrowed to one lane, with the truck on one side and a cliff on the other side. We asked the truck driver to stay put until all of the guys could push our vehicle beyond the truck and back on the slick and muddy road. I knew Dennis would come in handy.

By this time it was one o'clock in the morning. We continued on in a deathly silence, praying. Rain pelted the windshield as the wipers kept the rhythm of our rapidly beating hearts. The traffic had cleared but the heavy snow grew deeper and fog thicker.

Kenney pulled over and walked to my van for a meeting of the minds. As he leaned through the window I said, "Buddy, I've made a mistake. We shouldn't have tried this."

I was proud of Kenney's determination. "Franklin, we're both country boys. We know how to drive in the mountains and snow." Kenney knew it was not like me to claim defeat, but he had no way of knowing the weight I carried to think that the folks with us had entrusted me with their care.

"Franklin, it's gonna be alright. You've always said that if God sends us to a place, we have to go in His strength." I couldn't disagree. "Okay, let's do it."

We began our descent to the bottom of the mountain. Visibility was zero heading toward the valley floor. We were lost. Because of the heavy fog and snow, Kenney admitted he didn't really know where we were.

When we came to an intersection at the stop sign, Kenney turned right, but immediately questioned his decision. Mike MacIntosh, at the time senior pastor of Horizon Christian Fellowship in San Diego, was in the front passenger seat of Kenney's vehicle and began leading the other passengers in prayer as Kenney tried to get his bearings.

Over the left of Kenney's shoulder he saw something twinkling—a little red light. Kenney motioned for us to backup and redirected us toward the faint blink of the light—it was a French UN Peace Keeper checkpoint. At night, they were in charge of blockading the road that went across the airport. We finally knew our location and understood why the oncoming traffic had dwindled—the road had been closed. On the other side of the runway there were at least one hundred cars waiting to get through; cars that would have to wait until dawn for clearance.

Kenney rolled his window down to speak to the officer who said in French, "Road closed. Wait 'til morning." "We're all foreigners," Kenney said, "and we have to get to the city tonight."

With his flashlight glaring, the officer approached my vehicle, "Sir, you're approaching enemy forces. You shouldn't be here; it's very dangerous." I looked into the very kind face of the officer who seemed to realize we were determined to get through. I explained why it was vital we make it to our destination. He asked for our passports to verify our citizenship and he was convinced we were foreigners; he just didn't know to what extent. Our little group was made up of some who had never been out of the United States before, but what he may not have known was that we were all in the care of our great and mighty God.

GOD ON THE MOUNTAIN

The officer signaled to the guy at the gate up ahead and motioned us onward to one sentry post and then another; each allowing us through. We maneuvered through the deserted streets of Sarajevo, engulfed by an eerie silence. Buildings stood like skeletons in the darkness, and sporadic streetlights lit the snow-covered ruins. A sniper's bullet pierced the blackness, reminding us that the newly won peace was fragile.

We soon found ourselves winding down Sarajevo's main street—Sniper Alley—so named because opposing forces were stationed on either side. On a concrete wall, amidst a collage of graffiti, were the words in large, red letters WELCOME TO HELL.

Daylight was only a few hours off, so those of us who were driving gunned the accelerators to get through the boulevard of Sniper Alley. We were thankful and relieved to finally see the partially bombed out sign of where we would sleep that night, the Holiday Inn, encircled by the once-proud Olympic rings. It didn't matter to us that the whole front of the hotel had been blown off and was covered with heavy plastic. What did matter was that God had brought us through the mountain pass and guided us to the door of rest.

Looking out the window of my room that night, I knew that what had made the trip particularly hard and dangerous for us (the extreme fog) had also been the very thing that the Lord used to protect us from gunfire; we couldn't see anything and neither could the snipers. But we were never out of the eye of God.

We stayed in Sarajevo two nights and kept busy with distributions. We stopped on the street to talk with a young boy. When he learned that we were Americans he responded, "America is very beautiful. I hope to live there one day." Someone asked why he would want to leave his home. "Look around you," he replied, pointing to the bombed-out buildings around him. "There is nothing for me here." He was only twelve years old; this is why we had come. Our mission was to bring the hope of God's truth in the name of Jesus Christ.

Ricky and I asked if there was an evangelical church in the city. We were told that there was only one small church with a handful of members. The pastor and his wife were deeply discouraged. They had suffered greatly due to the war. We went to their little home and Ricky asked if we could pray with them, but "first," Ricky asked the pastor, "Can I wash your feet?"

Ricky said later that this dear pastor had carried the Gospel faithfully with so little results (that he was aware of). The man was taken aback as Ricky knelt and tenderly washed the feet of a faithful servant who had proclaimed the Gospel in hostile surroundings. Observing Ricky at that moment was one of the most meaningful examples of following in the footsteps of Jesus.

For years, the world had prayed for an end to the violent Balkan conflict, and for peace. But lasting peace will not be found through military intervention or the signing of peace accords. True peace is only found in the Prince of Peace, Jesus Christ, who died for our sins and rose again that we might have eternal life. The Bible says, "For He is our peace, who made both groups one and tore down the dividing wall of hostility" (Eph. 2:14 HCSB).

One of the most memorable distributions was at a school where seven hundred children were seated all the way up the steps. Ricky, Sharon, and Dennis played and sang while the children came alive with laughter, clapping, and cheering.

The team was keyed up when I went to the platform to speak, but Mary wanted to sing a song, with Ricky and Dennis accompanying her. Well, this was quite a scene. How many hillbilly singers, as Mary calls herself, were fortunate enough to have Grammy award musician Ricky Skaggs and the fastest flat-pick guitarist Dennis Agajanian playing for her?

If only the entertainment journalists could have been there to see that! Mark DeMoss, Tommy Coomes, and I decided to be Mary's backup singers. Ricky was accustomed to being on the stage with other professionals of the Grand Ole Opry. But humbly, he and Sharon traded the limelight of country music halls for five days in war-infested Bosnia.

When I asked Ricky what he thought of us amateurs he said, "Awe Franklin, the kids loved it and y'all sung your hearts out for them. I thought about all the people back at home who packed these little shoeboxes. What an investment they've made in the children of Bosnia. You know, the Lord didn't tell us to become grown-ups to enter the kingdom of Heaven, did He? He said that we've got to become like little children. It's just so precious to see how God's love can work through a little child," Ricky said. "Any music would make them happy!"

So there we were on stage performing "God on the Mountain." The kids were cheering and ecstatic, so it helped cover up our mistakes. However, the words Mary sang had a special meaning for all of us on the team because it was the same song that Mary had sung a couple of nights before when we were all maneuvering the narrow pass across Mount Igman.

> For the God on the mountain is still God in the valley
> When things go wrong, He'll make them right
> And the God of the good times
> Is still God in the bad times
> The God of the day is still God in the night.

Mary stood in front of these children whose lives had been ripped apart by things they could simply not understand, but somehow they understood the message of that song. The team couldn't help but remember the dangerous trip across the mountain, but that only lasted a short time. These children had lived with the reality of death, day after day. But that day, they learned about God who would be with them through the dark days and bad nights, even on the backside of that ominous mountain.

There may have only been one accessible road in and out of that battered city, but the Gospel message proclaimed that day showed them another road, another way—the road called hope. For Jesus said, "I am the way, the truth, and the life. No one comes to the Father except through Me" (John 14:6 HCSB).

COUNTING TO THREE!

We had come to bring hope, to dry the tears, and to put smiles on the children's faces. I took the microphone and told the Christmas story and explained that the gifts signified God's love for them. As the gifts were distributed, I told them to hold on to the boxes until every child had one. "When I count to 'three' you can open your presents."

The children listened and obeyed, but there was an undertone, a vibration of thrill on the brink of explosive joy. They were overcome with agonizing excitement and lack of patience. The expectation was so endearing. But the least I could do was to start counting: One . . . Two . . . Three!

The kids were wired—keyed up—high strung—frenzied. It was fabulous. We stood and soaked in the thrill of the moment, watching the sea of children ripping open their boxes. Some cried; others, like Mary, got right in the midst of the children and jumped around with them.

There wasn't much being said; the laughter, the giggling, and the squealing at an all-time pitch, reverberated on high. I stood just taking it in, and then began to mingle, showing the kids how to turn things on or wind things up. Some would reach up and say *"F-au-la . . . F-au-la . . . F-au-la!"* (Thank you). Hugs, embraces, even some kisses, said it all.

From Camels to Tents

"Thank you" is a common response from shoebox recipients. And we, too, are thankful to those who help make it all possible. Our team also heard it many times as they distributed gifts in the Middle East.

The Gospel came to the Holy Land first, because this is where the Christmas Child was born. But in the ancient days, the people resisted and rejected the gift of Jesus, and today not much has changed. However, the Bible lands are still close to the heart of God.

Samaritan's Purse brought the Gospel back to the Land of the Bible through the delivery of gift-filled shoeboxes. Our longtime ministry partner Aileen Coleman has delivered these gifts to children across the deserts, including al-Ruwayshid, Jordan, a remote village near the Iraqi border. Boys and girls at the primary school squealed with delight as they opened their gifts and found toys, school supplies, and other surprises inside.

Aileen, founder and director of the Annoor Hospital in Mafraq, has been serving the people of the Middle East for six decades. God has used the project to open doors for sharing the Good News with tent-dwelling Bedouin people who often live on the fringes of Jordanian society. "Even adults get excited when the kids receive their gifts," Aileen told us. "I'm grateful to Samaritan's Purse for giving us a way to reach children, and even the parents, with God's love."

These shoeboxes were carried to children on the backs of camels and donkeys. Many Bedouin tribes to this day live in caves or goat-haired tents and roam the land, much like they did in the days of Abraham, leading their flocks of sheep and goats from water hole to water hole. In spite of the fact that Bedouins live in the barren desert, they love bright colors and the packages brought excitement and thrill.

Skip and Lenya Heitzig once again led a team to this part of the world to assist Aileen with this monumental task. Delivering shoebox gifts in the desert is no easy task, but Skip and Lenya always see the bright side of the desert—they're from Albuquerque. My sister Ruth Graham also joined them and told me later it was the thrill of a lifetime to watch the kids open their gifts and hear them express such deep gratitude.

But even with all of this help, the task could not have been done without the advice and assistance from a member of the Jordanian Royal family. She is not only a dear friend to Aileen, but she has become a friend to Samaritan's Purse. In fact, she is our Good Samaritan in Jordan. She helped gain permission for our planes to land and assisted in finding a host of volunteers who were willing to help us. She loves Operation Christmas Child and the happiness it brings to the children. She has personally delivered thousands of shoeboxes over the years and continues doing so even as we write this book.

While the team was there, a little boy approached the ladies. He was excited. In one hand he held a worn-down pencil; in the other hand he held up a pack of brand new pencils that had come from his shoebox. He had never seen so many new pencils at once—all brightly colored. He whispered, "I counted fourteen pencils in my box. Do I have to give them back?" The women smiled and assured him that they were his to keep . . . all of them.

Even the cartons that the shoeboxes were packed in were valuable to these children. One eight-year-old girl started home with one of these large cartons balanced on her head. When asked what she would do with it, she had many ideas—a place for her baby brother, or a place to keep lambs warm when her family brings them into their cave at night.

Aileen pointed out, "To children who have nothing, everything is a treasure. These gifts reflect the heart of God who gave everything—His treasure to the world."

THE KEY IN OUR HAND THAT UNLOCKS HEARTS

We finished 1995 on a high plane—five of them—and our spirits were high as we soared into 1996 triumphant. We had been successful in mobilizing and training volunteers to sort the boxes by age and gender. This step alone improved our distributions by leaps and bounds, helping us feel more organized packing, collecting, and distributing shoeboxes.

We had a memorable distribution at the army concert hall in Sarajevo as we returned again to Bosnia. But the distribution that stands out is the one led by my good friend and pastor from Beirut, Lebanon, Sami Dagher.

Samaritan's Purse has worked with Sami in the Middle East for many years. Six years before 9/11, Sami led our team into Iraq with boxes. The very next year Sami mobilized a massive distribution in communities throughout Lebanon. Christians there had been praying that doors would open to the Gospel.

The Antonov 124 touched down at the Beirut International Airport loaded with shoebox gifts. Sami and his Karantina Church had paved the way for teams to visit orphanages, hospitals, homes and churches in and around the great city that sits on the slopes of the Mediterranean Sea.

Sami told the teams to use the shoebox gift as "a key in your hands" to unlock hearts to Jesus. This is exactly what happened on a visit to the refugee camp housing thousands of Palestinians. While all shoeboxes are special, a particular box had come from one of America's most beloved presidents. Former President Reagan and his wife Nancy had packed a box that was given away that day to a young mother who lived on the outskirts of Beirut in a place called Dbye.

Imagine a gloomy environment, a dingy home pelted by shrapnel, with rocket fire blasting in the dark lonely night. This was life for many children—this was the picture of Lebanon in the latter part of the twentieth century.

Carrying out a distribution of gifts was not an easy task for Sami's team, but it was certainly memorable as they navigated small alleyways and open sewage canals to reach a squalid, two-room dwelling that housed eight people.

The team was introduced to a young mother named Delil, barely fourteen. The tiny baby she cradled in her arms, Miliana, was just nine days old. The team explained to Delil that the gift was from President Reagan. Her face lit up as she lifted the lid and found among the array of gifts, clothing and little shoes for an infant girl, not to mention the iconic gray stuffed elephant.

During the visit, Delil's older brother, a crack addict, walked into the room. He was overwhelmed by the love shown to his sister and her child and sat down while the story of the Christmas Child was read. The young man was spellbound to hear that God had sent the greatest gift to mankind in the form of a baby. The Babe in the manger had become a refugee when the angel of the Lord told Joseph to take the Child and His mother and flee into another land to escape death.

This account impacted Delil's brother and before the team left, they led him to Christ. Material gifts may cause the recipient's eyes to open widely in fascination, but it is the magnificent Gospel that opens wide the door of the human heart, letting the light of God's truth cleanse and restore hearts that have fled far from Him.

Sami also told of a family who had expressed interest in a children's Bible for their son. When Sami went with the team to a Lebanese school, this little boy opened his shoebox and found a copy of the Bible in the Arabic language.

Can you imagine God directing a family in an English-speaking country to put an Arabic Bible in a shoebox (not knowing where it was going)? Then out of five million boxes, it was packed, sent to a processing center, sealed and put onto a pallet, and then shipped in a container across the ocean, ending up in Beirut, Lebanon (of all places), and eventually in the hands of this boy?

Stories like this confirm that shoeboxes are tools in God's hand. We pack them; God guides them, one by one.

All Things Great
And Small

One is a very small number; unless, of course, it stands before the mighty word "million." The number "one" seems insignificant unless you are talking about one Antonov 225, the largest plane ever to take to the air.

Most of us these days would not bend our knee to pick up one fallen penny, but if it were the 1943 Lincoln penny mistakenly struck in bronze and worth over one million dollars, I feel sure we would fall to the ground and rescue it back into our care. One suddenly becomes very great.

So when you see a child sitting in a trash heap in Guatemala, remember—that one child was created by God who values that little soul worth more than silver and gold. In fact, the Bible says that one soul is worthy of the priceless blood shed by the Savior of the world.

One person all alone can easily be overlooked, until you consider this: "It is the same in Heaven," Jesus said when looking for one lost coin or one lost lamb, "there is rejoicing among the angels of God over one sinner whose heart is changed [through repentance]" (Luke 15:10, Phillips).

Many ask, "Why a shoebox?" Try this on for size: "How beautiful . . . are the feet of him who brings good news, who proclaims peace, who brings glad tidings of good things, who proclaims salvation" (Isa. 52:7).

Shoes in a shoebox don't get very far, so why not step up to the challenge? Find that shoebox collecting dust way back in the closet, dump the shoes out and fill it up, wrap it up, cover it with prayer and walk it into a post office or partnering church and send it to Operation Christmas Child. Your shoebox can travel to places you will probably never go. It can wind up at the feet of a little child who is looking down, when he or she needs to be looking up. Through a simple shoebox, you can send good news—the Gospel of Jesus Christ—to a little one who may have never heard His name. Will your feet symbolically carry the Good News to the least of these? If so, you have just discovered the heart of Operation Christmas Child.

Spelling "Gospel" Starts with GO

Why do you need one more shoebox?" This question is asked all the time. Here's the answer: Until the Lord returns, there is one more soul that needs to be rescued—one more lamb that needs to be carried back into the fold. We call the largest international Christmas program for children in the world an "operation"—a rescue mission—to win souls for the Christmas Child, one little lamb at a time.

The soul is a precious and valuable treasure worthy of care. We cannot see it. We cannot touch it, but we can certainly feel its tug and pull. The psalmist cried out, "My soul melts from heaviness . . . for there is no one who acknowledges me; refuge has failed me; no one cares for my soul" (Pss. 119:28; 142:4). But God does, and He wants to use our feet, hands and lips in service to others.

God says, "All souls are Mine" (Ezek. 18:4). The Christmas Child—the Lord Jesus Christ—was sent to rescue lost souls. He proclaimed, "For the Son of Man has come to seek and to save that which was lost" (Luke 19:10). He comes for us individually. He knows our names. He calls our names. The question we must all answer is: Do we know His name; do we hear His call?

When Jesus finished His earthly ministry and returned to Heaven, His work did not cease. He broadened the scope of His ministry to mankind by sending the power of His Holy Spirit to boost our resolve, to deepen our faith, to put within us His heart. He put into the hands of His followers the commission to proclaim His message to the lost: the orphans, the widows, the sick, the disabled, the lonely, the poor, the discouraged and disadvantaged—the lost. Many children overseas have never heard His name—Jesus.

His great command comes from the first two letters of the Gospel. He has told us to "Go." Go where? To the ends of the earth.

So while we look back and give thanks for what God has done these past twenty years, we do it in the spirit of thanksgiving for His faithfulness, determined to keep "going" to those who do not yet know Him.

Operation Christmas Child reaches out to those in the state of famine, the state of war, and the state of calamities for one reason: the state of the soul.

One soul is of great worth to his Maker. Jesus spoke of the value of a soul and told the disciples that no man could ever have enough wealth to buy back his soul (Matt. 16:26).

The Psalms describe the state of the soul:

The soul is a parched land (143:6).

The soul is hungry and thirsty, and faints (107:5).

The soul melts because of trouble (107:26).

The weary say:

My soul clings to the dust (119:25).

My soul faints for your salvation (119:81).

My soul has dwelt too long with one who hates peace (120:6).

Bring my soul out of trouble (143:11).

Deliver my soul from death (116:8).

This is the most concise description of children in the darkest corners of our world. But Jesus paid the price of death with His life, to redeem what He had already created—the living soul—dead in trespasses and sin. His mission is to rescue and resurrect the soul from eternal death into eternal life.

LET THE CHILDREN COME

Children do not ask to be born. Yet one hundred and thirty million are born into the world annually (another forty-six million are aborted worldwide).

Some children are loved, some are rejected—abandoned.

Some children are treasured; others feel they have no worth.

Some children grow up in tranquility; others see nothing but terror.

Some children have homes; others no shelter at all.

Some children are educated; others cannot write their names.

Some children are secure; others long to be saved from harm.

But one thing they all have in common—all children have souls.

Why did Jesus say, "Let the little children come to Me"?

The answer is simple: because Jesus loves and values children. He values them so much that He became one Himself. His Father in Heaven sent Him at Christmas for one reason—to save mankind from sin. Each of us has entered this world as a child.

Jesus did not forget that He had come to this world as a Child and He taught that all who enter His kingdom would have to enter in child-like faith. In fact, this was a topic of conversation as Jesus walked with His disciples one day.

They must have been a considerable distance behind Him, because Scripture says that as they walked along the road they disputed among themselves who would be greatest in the kingdom of God.

When they reached their destination—a house in Capernaum—Jesus asked them what they had been discussing. "They kept silent."

Was it that they still hadn't learned that He knows the thoughts of the heart, or were they humiliated to be found out?

We can't say for certain, nor can we know exactly where they were in Capernaum, but this was the city where Peter lived; perhaps they were at Peter's house. Jesus had been there many times.

He was certainly among friends—His followers—yet they were arguing who would be the greatest in Heaven. Do you sometimes get irritated with the disciples when you read this passage? How could they even think such a thing, much less express it audibly, when they were in the very presence of the One who is King of Heaven?

But Jesus is going to teach them, and us, about being great. Imagine that He may have pulled a chair into the room to rest from the weary journey. The Bible says that Jesus "sat down, called the twelve, and said to them, 'If anyone desires to be first, he shall be last of all and servant of all'" (Mark 9:35).

Then He took a little child and set him in the midst of them. And when He had taken him in His arms, He said to them, "Unless you are converted and become as little children, you will by no means enter the kingdom of heaven. Therefore whoever humbles himself as this little child is the greatest in the kingdom of heaven. Whoever receives one little child like this in My name receives Me" (Matt. 18:3–5).

Can you just imagine a small child—perhaps one of Peter's—having Jesus in his home? Maybe he had been shooed away when Jesus entered the house. Nevertheless, Jesus called the child near and the child obeyed; perhaps even running to Jesus with his arms in the air and falling into His lap—happy to be recognized, to be wanted, to be called, to be loved.

Then the child feels the hands of Jesus lifting him up, drawing him close in the presence of these men.

Little children are trusting by nature. Why? Because they are helpless. They are dependent. They cannot do for themselves what a loving parent can do for them. Jesus knows that even adults cannot do His will without His help, and so He teaches by example to become as little children—humble, dependent, obedient.

I would imagine that the Twelve felt rather diminished as they gazed on the child who was embraced and loved by Jesus, but the message must not have stuck with them too long because a short time later, Jesus had to tell them again.

They had traveled to the region of Judea, by the other side of the Jordan. Multitudes had gathered to see Jesus. As was His custom, He taught them. Then people began bringing their little children to Jesus so that He would touch them and bless them.

Then Scripture makes a startling statement; "But the disciples rebuked those who brought them. But when Jesus saw it, He was greatly displeased and said to them, 'Let the little children come to Me, and do not forbid them; for of such is the kingdom of God' . . . and He took them up in His arms, laid His hands on them, and blessed them" (Mark 10:13–16).

There are times we get so caught up with protocol, procedures, rules, and regulations that we miss what the Lord is trying to teach us. This was the problem with the disciples. They saw the children coming to Jesus and told them to go away; they did not think the children were worthy of Jesus' attention.

We don't know how many there were, but if a multitude had come to hear Jesus, it is likely that the children made up quite a crowd themselves. Maybe when their parents grabbed their hands to take them to Jesus they were noisy, disturbing others, and the disciples were ticked off.

The disciples rebuked the parents, Jesus rebuked the disciples, and then instructed them to open the floodgate and let the children come to Him.

Jesus puts heavenly value on little children and this is why Samaritan's Purse reaches out to the least of these—to tell them about the love Jesus has for them. OCC shoebox gifts are the vehicles we use to get the message to them.

The Bible instructs that we are to teach children His commandments, His Word.

"Teach them diligently to your children . . . talk of them when you sit in your house, when you walk by the way, when you lie down, and when you rise up" (Deut. 6:7).

But what about the children who have no parents; who have no house?

To this the Bible answers, "Do justice to the fatherless and the oppressed" (Ps. 10:18).

Yes, children are valued by Jesus and we have an unprecedented opportunity through Operation Christmas Child to reach out and show them that they are loved by God.

What a miracle that the infant Moses was rescued from the Nile River. What a victory when David the shepherd boy slayed the giant. What a thrill to see Jesus take the boy's loaves of bread and fish and feed the hungry. Aren't we thankful that God sent the Christmas Child to perform the greatest operation on our darkened hearts and give us new life in Him?

Yes, Jesus does love the little children of the world—from every continent—they are precious in His sight.

SHOEBOXES AND DANDELION SEEDS

That's why people all over the country rummage through their closets, blowing the dust off shoeboxes, dumping their shoes on the floor, and wrapping boxes and lids separately in bright Christmas paper before filling them with everything from coloring books and crayons to trucks and baseballs, or little purses and mirrors.

The idea of reaching out to kids is packed with important steps, yet it is so simple.

Have you ever watched a child blow on a dandelion? Each single flower in a head is called a floret, known by many as the "blowing flower," because it produces many windborne seeds. When airborne, they scatter far and wide, making the "dandelion snow" almost impossible to catch. Children love them! And many mothers often receive them in fisted bouquets from their children.

Read about the dandelion sometime; you will find that this little field 'flower' grows all over the world. In Persian countries, for instance, the dandelion is called *qasedak*, meaning "small postman," because it is believed that seeds released in the air bring "good news."

I think of shoeboxes as blowing flowers, carrying the seeds of the Gospel far and wide. Children pack shoeboxes with fistfuls of gifts that are blown into the skies by jumbo jets. When the boxes settle on the ground, the seeds of God's love are deposited into little hearts.

"[The] seed . . . increased and produced: some thirtyfold, some sixty, and some a hundred" (Mark 4:8).

Happy Home Orphanage

Like the Christmas Child, "Vally" was found in a manger surrounded by animals and was rescued and brought to an orphanage sponsored by Samaritan's Purse.

Our team from England had gone to Romania with shoeboxes. Driving through desolate wasteland and making their way up the concrete drive to the first distribution, they arrived at Caminul Felix "Happy Home" orphanage. There were six pastel buildings and the bright colors were a happy contrast to the barren surroundings.

This is where they met six-year-old Valorica and heard her story. She had been found by Gypsies when she was an infant, in a coma and very weak. They cared for her and eventually brought her to "Happy Home," where she was able to find love and security—and a shoebox.

Gypsy children in northern Romania are not allowed to go to school until they can provide their own supplies. We've done many distributions among the Gypsy people and this is one of the greatest delights they receive: school supplies. Children do want to learn, they do want to go to school.

Mehi is such a child. When he opened his box and found paper, pencils, and markers, he ran through the village to his mother and said, "I have been given the best box in the whole village." He ran back to the organizers and shouted, *nais tuke* (Thank You!). Mehi shouted. "Now I can go to school."

His mother came to say thank you. To her surprise, she was given a bigger box than her son—it was an empty cardboard carton that had held shoeboxes. When the team saw her eyeing it, they understood how valuable cardboard would be to her and they gave it to her to take home. It was as though she had been given something of great value. When asked what she was going to do with the carton, she clasped her hands together and said, "This will be a rug in my house; it will keep our feet warm! *Nais tuke*."

In countries around the world, simple things mean everything. Not even cardboard is wasted.

Bosnia 1993: Ross and Carol Rhoads led the Red Team into war-ravaged Bosnia for the first Samaritan's Purse shoebox distribution.

Bosnia 1993: Stan Barrett, the first man to break the on-land sound barrier in a rocket car, joined the Red Team to deliver Christmas gifts to the children of war in Bosnia.

Bosnia 1993: Sean Campbell who directed the work of Samaritan's Purse—Canada in 1993 was part of the Red Team going into Bosnia just before Christmas.

1994: Greg Laurie's church, Harvest Christian Fellowship in Riverside, California, was one of the first to establish "Shoebox Sunday."

Rwanda 1994: Todd Chasteen contemplates the remarkable spirit of Rwanda's children.

Rwanda 1994: Pastor Skip and Lenya Heitzig from Calvary Chapel, Albuquerque, New Mexico, led our team into Rwanda months after the brutal slaughter of 500,000 people in 1994, leaving thousands of children orphaned. The shoeboxes brightened little faces.

Rwanda 1994: Kenney Isaacs was in and out of Rwanda in 1994 and returned with the distribution team to handout shoeboxes to grief-stricken children, the innocent victims of war.

Croatia 1994: My eldest son Will visits with two excited Croatian boys while on a shoebox distribution.

Stansted 1995: Making history. Five Antonov 124s loaded with Christmas boxes for children around the world!

Jordan 1995: My sister, Ruth Graham, joined our distribution team to deliver Christmas gifts and bring comfort to little ones—many who had never received a gift.

Jordan 1995: Aileen Coleman (right) and a member of the Jordanian Royal Family (left), a longtime friend of Aileen's, deliver shoebox gifts to Bedouin families in the desert of Jordan.

Iraq 1995: Sami Dagher inspects the cartons of shoeboxes given in Jesus' name but confiscated by Saddam Hussein—however God's plan was not diverted.

Bosnia 1995: When I could not get a response from a little boy after delivering a shoebox gift, I called Mary Damron to the boy's bedside. Though Mary could not speak the local language, she managed to get through to the boy and the visit ended with laughter and joy.

Bosnia 1995: I found a little girl who had been injured during the war in Bihac, Bosnia, to receive the shoebox gift President Bill Clinton packed at the request of Mary Damron following a visit to the White House.

Bosnia 1995: Ricky Skaggs and wife Sharon White joined me on the infamous trip into Bosnia. After a treacherous trip across Mount Igman, several distributions were held in and around Sarajevo where Ricky and Sharon performed for hundreds of children.

Mexico 1997: Following Hurricane Mitch, Veronica Pomeroy was invited to join our team in Honduras in 1997 to hand out gifts. She and her army of friends packed and collected 1,400 shoeboxes. The twelve-year-old girl with cystic fibrosis continued to collect thousands of shoeboxes until her death at the age of twenty-two. "She wanted others to understand the importance of giving," her mom said.

Haiti 1997: My son Roy has made numerous trips to handout Christmas boxes to children. Here he enjoys visiting with some children in Haiti.

Mexico 1997: Jim Harrelson, vice president of OCC, is great with kids. Here in Mexico he helped explain the letter to this child who was thrilled with everything in the box.

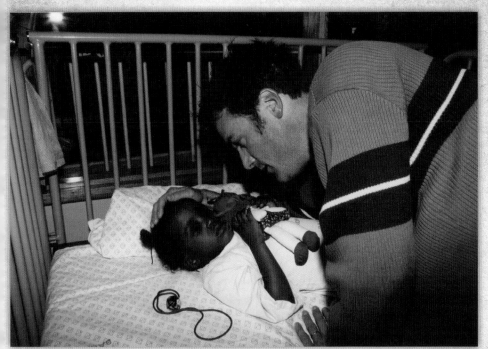
South Africa 1997: Michael W. Smith tenderly comforts a little patient with no eyes in Soweto's pediatic cancer center.

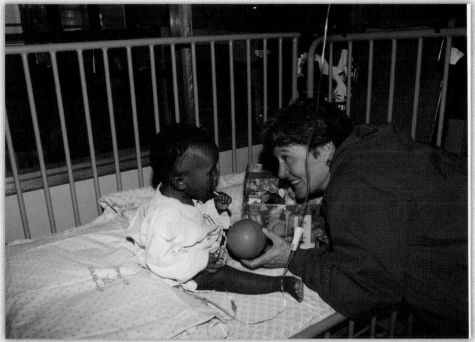
South Africia 1997: My wife, Jane Austin, captures the attention of a little one enjoying some treats from the shoebox gift during a visit to a hospital outside of Johannesburg.

Long Beach, California 1998: Louis (Louie) Zamperini came to be with me at Long Beach International Airport before an OCC press conference. Louie is a former American Olympic distance runner and World War II prisoner of war (POW). Following his rescue, he was saved at a Billy Graham Crusade in Los Angeles in 1949.

Kosovo 1998: Cliff Barrows enjoys a precious moment with one of the Kosovo children.

Honduras 1999: Accompanied by a stuffed musical lamb, an idea of my mother Ruth Bell Graham, I sang "Jesus Loves Me" to young Juni at the Sendero de Amor or "Path of Love" orphanage in Honduras.

Honduras 1999: Helicopters are often used to transport cartons of shoebox gifts to waiting children fascinated by the chopper in the sky.

Central Asia 2001: Donkeys are sure-footed when it comes to rough terrain. This little guy is surely content riding on the beast of burden.

Vietnam 2002: With help from sighted friends, students at a Hanoi school for the blind enjoyed shoebox gifts distributed through our Vietnamese partners.

New York 2002: At the OCC Press Conference in the Big Apple. (Right to left): My son Edward, Edward's brother-in-law Dave Webb and Winston Lawson (in beige overcoat) who was the secret service agent in charge of security when President Kennedy was assassinated in Dallas, Texas. Win Lawson is probably the most famous and most respected of the secret service agents and a close friend of mine. Senator Bill Frist addressed the crowd just a short distance from Ground Zero.

New York 2002: International Recording Artist Bono talks Operation Christmas Child with an enthusiastic supporter.

Uganda 2002: First Lady of Uganda, Janet Museveni, wife of Uganda's president, joined the OCC team for a distribution to children who have lost parents due to AIDS. Many of these gifts were given by New York City policemen and firefighters after 9/11.

Afghanistan 2002: These "ships of the desert" provide a unique form of transportation for shoebox gifts.

Sudan 2003: This boy is fortunate that he doesn't have to share his bed with another sick child at the crowded hospital in North Khartoum, Sudan.

Sudan 2003: Jack Kippenberger, retired secret service agent, helps unload shoebox gifts for children in Sudan. He traveled with me to many parts of the world before his death in 2010.

Cambodia 2004: Children wait patiently—but expectantly—for the count to three!

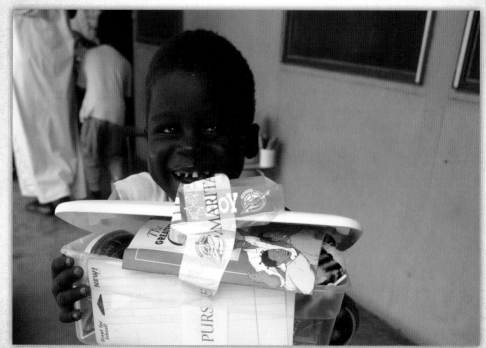
Sudan 2004: Christmas gifts lifted the spirits of this disabled boy. Polio—eradicated in most of the world—still affects thousands of children in Southern Sudan.

THE SHOEBOX LADY EVANGELIZES
IN SHOE STORE

✳

I stayed so busy with shoeboxes I didn't realize I was growing old." That's what Doris Goodair, a seventy-three-year-old lady from Mission, British Columbia, said long after she started packing shoeboxes for Operation Christmas Child. She never wasted an opportunity to be a witness for Christ. When Doris heard me interviewed on television about OCC, she got busy collecting shoeboxes. Her home literally became a shoebox shop that was operational year-round.

With each passing year, Doris increased her number of shoe-boxes, eventually collecting over forty-two hundred and she became known as the "Shoebox Lady." When Doris ran out of room in other parts of the house, her husband Bud gave up some of his own space and even donated the sale of a boat to pay the overseas shipping cost of the shoeboxes.

Doris's vision was motivated by her personal relationship with Jesus Christ. She wanted others to find the peace that only comes from salvation in Him. I found her story interesting because her spirit of giving began, you might say, years ago in a shoe store on Christmas Eve.

A young man walking along the sidewalk caught Doris's eye. His shoes were so worn that his toes were sticking out. She couldn't pass by without helping. She and Bud marched him over to a shoe store and bought him a pair of boots. He left the store that evening with more than just a pair of boots; the box under his arm represented the Gospel that would set feet walking on a new pathway, all because Doris's feet were shod with the Gospel of peace.

For Doris and Bud, it just seemed natural to get on board the OCC Express—and how faithful they were. They exemplified our theme that year; pack it up, send it up, light it up. Doris passed away in 2009, but she had been used to light up others' lives with the Gospel.

GIFTS OF HOPE IN GERMANY

Shortly before Christmas at my father's meeting with the Billy Graham Evangelistic Association (BGEA), I spoke to his domestic and international staff about Operation Christmas Child and showed our video, which had been received with enthusiasm around the country and on television.

My father's executive director in Berlin, Germany, at the time, Dr. Irmhild Baerend, also serves as Editor of *Entscheidung*, Germany's version of *Decision* (BGEA Christian magazine) and asked permission to write an article about OCC.

Just after the article appeared in one of the 1996 issues in Germany, sixteen hundred shoeboxes arrived in our Berlin office. Irmhild called with excitement and surprise, and before we knew it, OCC had dug some roots in German soil.

Our international teams in Australia, Europe, and North America are made up of dedicated ambassadors that have mobilized prayer warriors around the world. We have watched God bring individuals to this ministry, in support roles and leadership roles, with hearts to serve Him and we thank and praise the Lord for enabling them in their tasks.

Jesus Is "Numbair" One

More than twenty-five thousand churches in the United States alone had come alongside Samaritan's Purse in 1997, and worldwide, twenty thousand volunteers donated their time. Time is a precious commodity not taken lightly.

I had been scheduled to preach festivals in South Africa. We started in Cape Town and finished in Johannesburg. Michael W. Smith had joined me on that trip and the team had organized a shoe-box distribution at the pediatric cancer ward at a hospital in Soweto. A dread hung over us as we arrived; many had never been to a cancer ward filled with young patients.

But having Michael and Dennis Agajanian along to play their guitars helped brighten faces; that is until Michael approached the bed of a toddler. When he got close, Michael realized she had no eyes. He put his guitar aside and wiped the tears from his own eyes. There would be no song from him at that bedside.

My wife, Jane Austin, and daughter Cissie stood there with Michael, brokenhearted for this little child. But as Jane began to unpack the child's box, there was a sense of knowing the gifts would bring a little cheer—like the little duck that quacked—and it did.

Michael and Dennis were in need of a little cheer themselves; so the timing was good when the hospital administrator approached me and said, "Mr. Graham, the children would like to thank you for what you have done today. They've been practicing a song to say, 'thank you.' May we assemble your team in the corridor for the children's presentation?"

I looked over at Michael and Dennis and said, "Guys, you're being replaced!"

They moved aside as the children poured into the hallway from wards throughout the hospital. There was no dread; this place came alive with the happy sound of music from a group of joyful kids. They were prepared. They were excited. They couldn't wait to say, "thank you."

With powerful voices and electrifying smiles, they performed a local favorite: *Jesus Is Number One.* Swaying to the strong African beat and shaking their fingers to make their point, they belted out in an Afrikaans' accent, "No matter what the people say, Jesus is 'numbair' One." The enthusiasm was magnetic.

Others began to pour into the area: doctors, nurses, and soon all the spectators were clapping their hands with the children. Michael and Dennis were coaxed into the choir to join them and when they concluded, there were smiles, hugs, and joy.

We spent the rest of that trip rehearsing the beat, the tune, and the words. In fact, long after I got home I found myself in step with that wonderful truth: Jesus is Number One.

This is the message that accompanies the shoebox—it is the miracle message—and "the one and only" message carried to children around the world in a simple shoebox. We left that place hearing a choir of "thank-yous" resounding as we walked through the exit doors and into a world most of the kids would never see again.

"Heart" Felt Thanks

Born out of Operation Christmas Child was a program called the Children's Heart Project (CHP). After all, our purpose was to spread the Gospel in order that hearts might be changed. In doing so, we learned of so many children in developing countries desperately in need of heart surgery. This was the case of thirteen-year-old Nasiha Bucuk. She had outlived her life expectancy, and the treatment she desperately needed was not available in her home country's war-ravaged hospitals.

Samaritan's Purse began exploring the possibility of bringing children to the United States and Canada, engaging hospitals and surgeons to donate their skills and services to help children who would otherwise have no hope of reaching adulthood.

We flew Nasiha, her mother, and a translator to South Carolina. Surgeons at the Medical University Hospital performed open-heart surgery and within days, Nasiha was more active than she had been in a long time and expressed heartfelt thanks.

Since this project began in 1997, nine hundred and forty-three children from fourteen countries have received this life-saving surgery. From an open shoebox to open-heart surgery, hearts are being opened to the Giver of life and the Great Physician—His name is Jesus.

The Children's Heart Project has been instrumental in seeing many patients, family members, and translators come to Christ and their spiritual hearts have been transformed. They return to their countries with hope for the future, and often become one-on-one witnesses to others about how God heals and transforms hearts.

This is what keeps us engaged in exploring new horizons beyond the box and beyond the end of another happy year.

Orphaned and Abandoned, but Not Forgotten

The Bible tells us to open our ears to the cries of the needy. We are also instructed to care for the orphans. Just how many orphans or abandoned children are in the world? There's no easy answer. Some define an orphan as a child having lost one parent; others define an orphan as losing both mom and dad. Regardless of the number, whether one hundred forty-three million or thirteen million, the Bible instructs us to "look after orphans in their distress" (James 1:27 NIV).

I have been to orphanages around the world, and none of them measure up to what most of us call home—a safe refuge—and a place where mom is there to comfort the hurts of her child, or where a father provides protection. But thank God there are orphanages that welcome those on the outside, in.

What would you do if you opened your door and found a small child on your doorstep? This happens all the time in many parts of the world, and it happened in a village not far from Moscow. Five-year-old Ivan was dropped off at the front door of the Kosterovo Children's Home. His hands were tied together and a note pinned to his shirt saying, "I don't want him, he's yours now."

We are thankful for people who care enough to take lost children in and care for them. Our teams work closely with our partners who develop relationships with orphanages, hospitals, and other future distribution sites before we send one shoebox.

Laying a strong foundation is a biblical principle and critical for an ongoing work such as OCC. Because we do work with government institutions, a strong follow-up process is imperative. We want to ensure that the gifts given will not be taken away from the children once our teams are gone. It is always heartbreaking to do distributions in orphanages where there is no Christian influence, but these are the kids, especially, who need to learn of God's love for them, and we are thankful that He allows us to walk through these doors.

WOW! JUST FOR ME?

S uch is the heart-rending story of Vladimir "Ted" Foreman who
was born in Russia and grew up emotionally broken, with no
hope. Like so many children in Russia, his parents were alcoholics,
so at three years old he and his two sisters joined four hundred other
young residents at a government-run home for orphans.

"Every child felt the same sense of loss," Ted said, "We knew we
were not loved. The daily routine was a mass production; the staff
was there to earn money to take home to their families, so the bare
minimum was done for us."

It is not unusual for children to be placed in one orphanage and
about the time they feel acclimated, they are moved to another, often
being separated from siblings. Many cannot hope for the future
because they have no sense of the past. As Ted said, "There was no
sense of possession."

Ted and his twenty roommates shared many things: one bath
a week in dirty water, one towel never clean or dry, and a dreadful
existence accompanied by hungry stomachs and lonely hearts.

He remembers being taken to an orthodox church on occasion.
He hoped to find some connection there. "I remember talking to the
priest and he gave me a list of rules I couldn't keep," Ted recounted.
"I began to doubt that religion could help me with my problems. I
didn't know any god, and if there was a god, he would not care about
me."

One day following a doctor's appointment, Ted returned to the
orphanage and immediately sensed a very different environment.
"Something is happening here," he reflected. But he wasn't sure how
to describe it until sometime later; it was joy.

When Ted walked into the classroom, he didn't notice the barren walls. Instead, the room lit up with colorful boxes on each desk. The place sparkled with sunshine, seen in the eyes and smiles of the children. Laughter put a thrill in the air. Voices filled the room with hope. "This had never happened before," he recalled.

Ted was reluctant to get too excited about the box, figuring that it would be given then taken away. But when he was convinced that it was his he thought, *Wow, somebody really packed this just for me?* That someone outside his life would care was unimaginable. Ted continued:

> The box was filled with things I never thought I would possess. But what meant the most was the toothpaste. It smelled so good—like bubble gum—so I ate the entire tube at once. It filled the hole in my stomach. Then I found a brand new towel. I learned later it was called a washcloth, but we never had towels like Americans—a washcloth, a hand towel, a bath towel, a decorative towel. In Russia, a towel is a towel. To think I could own my own personal towel was more than I could have ever hoped for and I cherished and guarded it because it belonged to me.
>
> I didn't hear about Jesus Christ that day because I was late to the party, but the seed of hope was born in me the day the shoebox came and I was determined to find out about the One who loved me so much.
>
> In time, my sisters and I were adopted by a couple in Minnesota and I had a family who loved me. At first, the only way my dad and I could communicate was for him to type something in English and then the computer would translate for me. One day I went down to the basement where my dad was working. He could tell I wanted to "talk," so using this high-tech form of communication he typed, "Hey Ted, now that you are in America and have a family who loves you, are you truly happy?"
>
> The question surprised me. Of course I'm happy. How could I not be happy with all the good that had happened

to me? But I sat back and thought about the answer and concluded that there really was something bigger than this. As awesome as family is, there had to be something more. I believed that if I could discover the source of hope, it would fill up the "empty place" still deep inside.

I tried to explain this to my dad. That's when he shared the Gospel with me. He did it so simply. As I tried to process this revelation, I remembered the difference the shoebox had made in my life—and the sense of hope it brought. It was a free gift but I had to receive it not fearing that it would be taken away. Now I knew the One who had provided the gift—His name is Jesus. And He came into my life through a simple gift that someone had packed and sent in His name. At that moment, my life was transformed. In fact, my parents would have said that I did a 180—I was a changed boy.

The hope that I felt for years was now defined in Christ, the source of hope—the God of hope. Realizing this mystery had been unlocked, I wanted to tell everybody. This became my next step along my journey of faith.

I learned to pray, asking God to help me share this great news. One morning I noticed my mom wearing a shirt with a familiar logo. My sisters and I looked at it and became so hyper that we talked a mile a minute—in Russian. Then we noticed the perplexed look on my parents' faces as if to say, "English please!"

Working out our recollections, we came to the same conclusion—the logo was exactly the same as what appeared on the tape that sealed the shoebox gifts—it hadn't changed over the years. This was Operation Christmas Child!

We learned that our parents had packed shoeboxes since 1995 and even wondered if they had packed the shoeboxes we received, but what excited us more was when they said we could pack boxes with them that very fall. "But you'll have to use some of your own money to buy the gifts."

That was okay with me. I only had $37, but nothing thrilled me more than to be on this side of the box; sending to a kid maybe just like me, who needed salvation in Christ. To think that God would use me—a broken vessel—to proclaim the greatest message of all, through OCC, is humbling and exciting.

The journey of a shoebox is a worthwhile trip, because often it leads the recipient into a better life—and the hope of Heaven.

WHAT A DIFFERENCE A STORM MAKES

On the other side of the world, a major distribution was done in Honduras at the Estadio Olympico in San Pedro Sula, Honduras. Weeks before, Hurricane Mitch had slammed into the country, flooding rivers that isolated the city of San Pedro Sula. Thousands were killed and thousands more left homeless.

The contrast from the year before was staggering. The 1997 Central America Olympic Games had been held with fifty thousand people filling the new and most prestigious athletic facility. Now, this same venue had become home to Hondurans displaced by the destructive power of the hurricane. Living under the concrete stands or in crudely constructed stalls arranged along the stadium walls, the victims faced a bleak holiday season.

But for several hours one December day, more than eight hundred children living in this complex enjoyed a memorable Christmas—the day Samaritan's Purse arrived. A spiritual fiesta was held and the Good News of the Gospel was shared with each child. They received not only shoebox gifts but Christian literature in their own language. Hearts were softened as many of the children put their toys aside to read the Christmas story.

We were not equipped at the time to develop our own Christian literature and were so grateful to discover a little booklet entitled *The Greatest Gift of All*, written for children. It told the story of Christ's birth and gave a clear presentation of the Gospel, explaining salvation. Colorful illustrations attracted children and this is what we were able to put into the hands of children that day in San Pedro Sula.

This was the reason for the season—to proclaim Christ.

This evangelistic storybook has been distributed around the world in eighty languages and has been used mightily by the Lord. The reaction from children has been astounding. One mother wrote later,

> Thank you for what you gave to my children—hope. We were devastated to lose our home and our jobs. My children stopped school. But when the shoeboxes came, their hearts started again and we have learned about the greatest gift that is Jesus and we hope for a new home in Heaven someday.

I'M NO SINGER

Whenever I saw my mother she wanted to know how the children were reacting to the musical lamb that plays "Jesus Loves Me." So when I returned from Honduras, I went to see her and showed her a picture of little Juni at the *Sendero de Amor* (Path of Love) orphanage.

"When I saw her," I told my mother, "I could almost hear you whisper, 'over there Franklin.' I kneeled beside the girl and placed one of your little lambs in her arms. She cuddled it. Then I wound it and put it up against her ear. Her little body calmed and her big eyes stared at me as if to say, 'Sing!'"

Now I'm no singer, but when this precious girl reached up to hug me, she put the music box to my ear and I sang the words, as she tightened her grip around my neck. Before leaving, we made sure that she had the words translated into Spanish so that not only the tune, but also the message, could bring joy and comfort to her little heart.

My mother loved the story and made sure that there was a flock of little musical lambs transported to every shoebox distribution.

"My lips shall greatly rejoice when I sing to You" (Ps. 71:23). ". . . little ones to Him belong, they are weak, but He is strong."

FEET THAT PREPARE THE WAY

Transporting the shoeboxes is a story almost as colorful as the boxes and is a massive operation that starts in our collection and processing centers. In 1999, our United States processing centers alone received help from nineteen thousand pairs of hands—and Daniel Ritchie's feet. Born without arms, this young man (fifteen years old at the time), was a joy to the entire team in Charlotte. What Daniel did have was a willing heart and a contagious smile. He came with a desire to use his feet to spread the Gospel around the world.

Many people have good reasons why they cannot do volunteer work, but for those who serve with us, their contribution is greatly valued. Our processing centers not only collect boxes; they collect stories from people around the world; and they always touch us as we hear about torches that are lit in giving hearts.

I'm thankful for the sensitive hearts of our staff and volunteers. They see more than just the shoeboxes. They are sensitive to those around them, constantly ready to bless others and be blessed by those who come from all walks of life and every circumstance imaginable.

So, our folks put Daniel to work. His coordination was amazing. He removed the rubber bands and inspected the items in the boxes and then put the lid back on. He also kept the warehouse staff on their feet because he worked so fast. They laughed and cried together, took breaks together, and when the work for the day was done, they sent him home with hugs and prayers, telling him that he had carried the Gospel with grace "having shod your feet with the preparation of the gospel of peace" (Eph. 6:15).

But the story within the story worth telling is about the unmatched volunteer base that God provides and uses to make OCC viable. This is an army that earns the right to demonstrate the heart of God. There is no question in our minds that the "God room" principle is very much at the heart of the outpouring of talent, desire, and sheer selflessness of people around the world who come to serve the Lord through OCC. This is not a job to them, it is a calling—a calling they answer and a calling to which they are committed. This is the body of Christ mobilized and operational.

Some come from the medical community, some from the sports world, and others from the creative arts. Some leave their credentials at home and roll up their sleeves to do whatever needs doing. Others come to help while on military leave or school break. There are men and women who retire early just so that they can come as often as they are needed. These folks are committed, enthused, and dependable. They come in forms of senior citizens, teenagers, grade school children, moms and dads. They come in motor homes, on planes, on motorcycles, in wheelchairs, on buses, in taxi cabs, on crutches, on canes and walkers, on bicycles, and on foot.

They are also the key to transporting these boxes from Canada, the United States, Australia, and our partnering European countries. This monumental task would be impossible without them.

It would also be impossible to put these gifts in the hands of children without the use of every form of transportation imaginable—as varied as the boxes themselves.

All over the world shoeboxes have been loaded on practical and primary modes of transportation. You don't have to flip through *National Geographic* to see stunning pictures of our four-legged transportation. Just get a copy of OCC materials and videos and you'll see animals doing something worthwhile—transporting shoeboxes:

> Camels in the Middle East—ships of the desert
>
> Pack mules in Africa—sure-footed beasts of burden
>
> Elephants in Asia—grand carriages for precious cargo
>
> Yaks in the Himalayans—supply caravans with round-cloven hooves

Shoeboxes have been airlifted by helicopters in Honduras, stacked inside dugout canoes in Papua New Guinea, piled up on horse-drawn wagons and rickshaws in Vietnam; loaded onto eighteen-wheelers in North America, hung over bicycles and motorcycles in Thailand, and balanced on the tops of heads.

And when nothing else is available, shoeboxes are strapped to the backs of volunteers whose hearts beat with the thrill of entering the most remote villages on foot with the Gospel.

OCC Seniors are Young at Heart

Kids love Operation Christmas Child and while it started with the idea of kids giving to kids, we quickly learned that it was just as much fun for adults.

Families work together at OCC, and some have to work extra hard to keep up with retirees who find great joy in packing boxes for kids.

Without conscious planning, people have seen that OCC has something for everyone to do and the older generations have given new meaning to "young at heart." It's interesting that the word "senior" is something to attain all through life. School kids can't wait to become high school seniors. Career oriented people look forward to attaining senior positions in their companies. But when folks retire, many aren't too happy to be called senior citizens.

I'm not sure what our ministries would do without the wonderful folks who come to help us. Growing up, I was taught to respect my elders. I learned a lot from some who were my parents' age and I spent a great deal of time with many of them traveling around the world. They were fun to be with and sometimes hard to keep up with. I thank God for what they bring to ministries like ours: wisdom, experience, and a strong sense of responsibility. They may fall into a category called senior citizens, but to us they are mighty special.

Graeme and Bette Pearson have been involved with OCC from the beginning and are great encouragers in our work. Graeme has served for years with Samaritan's Purse Australia as a member of our board of directors. When he retired as CEO of a large corporation, he and his wife were instrumental in helping to build OCC. Graeme traveled helping to identify countries where we could do distributions and Bette ran an OCC office out of their home. She was a great support to us (even allowing the ministry work to disrupt her home at times). Like all OCC start-ups, interest boomed, and after months of the overwhelming amounts of mail and receipting Bette handled, it was time to move the operation into an office where others could help. But those early years for OCC in Australia laid the groundwork for OCC in that part of the world. Some of the great testimonies of how shoeboxes have led children to salvation and how church planting have proven the value of the investment the Pearsons have made through the years.

This story can be repeated many times over in each of our sending countries. In the United States, the largest sending country, Randy Riddle, director of OCC Domestic, has been instrumental in developing our volunteer program. He has been with Samaritan's Purse since 1996 and has served with Operation Christmas Child almost from the beginning. He is a man who loves children and is one of the most enthusiastic supporters of our volunteers. I have always appreciated the fact that Randy invested himself in this army for the Lord and they, in turn, express their appreciation often for the fact that he helps them accomplish their hearts' desire—to be servants of Jesus Christ through OCC.

Ben and Linda Betzer are two such volunteers. They had retired on the same day, but they were certainly not ready to retire from serving the Lord. Praying diligently, they told the Lord they were prepared to put their hands to the plow and sow Gospel seed for His kingdom.

We were pleased that God led them to our Processing Center in Orange County, California. Since joining with us, they've just about done it all. Today, they serve as area coordinators, leading a team of seventy-five long-term volunteers; rarely do they lose one. Their joy is watching the team grow in their faith as God multiplies the fruits of their service.

Their daughter-in-law, who teaches at a Christian school, packs eight hundred boxes annually. Their daughter, also a teacher, began packing boxes and reached a goal of five thousand in 2012. Ben's brother, a pastor in Florida, shared the project with his congregation and they now pack four thousand boxes annually. A niece in South Carolina has caught the vision and started packing shoebox gifts. But that wasn't quite enough for the Betzers; they started an annual OCC packing party. This, of course, is in addition to their volunteer service. Their family tree blossoms with shoeboxes.

From the West Coast to the East Coast, to the Deep South, the Betzer family has watched God answer prayer, demonstrating that availability is a key component in serving God.

CARDBOARD SOLES

I asked my father's longtime friend and ministry partner Cliff
Barrows to lead a team to Kosovo along with Dr. Mel Cheatham,
former Ambassador Richard Capen, BGEA board member; BGEA
team member Henry Holley, and Jim Hodges.

"Uncle Cliff," as I call him, was part of the team who had traveled
around the world supporting my father as he proclaimed the Good
News at evangelistic meetings. But what he saw in Kosovo was unlike
anything he had ever seen. The bitter conflict had left thousands
dead and had driven thousands to seek asylum in Bosnia, Albania,
and other neighboring countries.

The team was taken to a school where children eagerly waited to
receive their shoeboxes. "The children were so well behaved," Cliff
remarked, "and were grateful for any small kindness done for them.
Children sat two per table and the gifts were handed out according
to age, youngest to oldest. One boy received his box while the boy
next to him waited for his age group. The younger opened his box
and said to the other, 'Here, you take what you want.' It spoke to
my heart to see the demonstration of brotherly love in a place that
exhibited tremendous conflict and strife."

Cliff recalled visiting an old warehouse where families had
found shelter. The ceiling dripped of cold water, and ice covered
the walkway. Sheets were crudely hung by families hoping for a
little privacy. But one little boy who lived there was very happy. He
had gotten a shoebox with brand new shoes that fit him perfectly.
"When he showed his mother, she cried," Cliff told me, "because that
very morning she had cut cardboard soles to fit his worn-out shoes.
When that mother learned that the shoeboxes were given in the

name of Jesus and read *The Greatest Gift of All* booklet, also given to her son, she gave her heart to Christ."

At a celebration of his ninetieth birthday in 2013, Cliff Barrows was still talking about that trip as one of the most moving experiences of his life saying, "I've never experienced anything quite like seeing the children who had been through so much tragedy respond so appreciatively to the story of Jesus Christ, and to see the joy of a simple gift."

THE BOX WITH THE COAT FINDS
ITS WAY TO THE BOY

K osovo had been ripped apart. Samaritan's Purse had taken a
giant step of faith by sending shoeboxes into Kosovo. In 1999
we had done the largest distribution in the history of Operation
Christmas Child, and the most daunting. We had worked in this
dangerous war zone complicated by mountainous terrain, winter
snows, cultural and religious conflicts, few evangelistic churches,
and virtually no government. The war had lasted fifteen months, but
it would be many years before the nation would be back on its feet.

Our Gospel infantry delivered gift boxes to schools and villages
throughout the country—with the goal of reaching every girl and boy
in Kosovo with tokens of God's love. We even went into Albania, a
country that had experienced freedom from one of the last European
Stalinist dictators, Enver Hoxha. In a land torn by centuries of strife,
an entire generation has been given a glimpse of Christ—the only
source of true peace and hope.

I had invited good friends of mine, Bill and Verna Pauls, to go
with me to Kosovo. Bill serves on the BGEA board of directors and
Verna was our first volunteer in the Rocky Mountain State. The
Lord used her to help us get OCC off the ground in Colorado. She
and Bill not only held events for OCC, but they provided office and
warehouse space in the Denver area. The three of us, along with a
couple of crew members, left Denver following a press conference
and flew to Shannon, Ireland, and then into Skopje, Macedonia. We
traveled from there by car into a ravaged land where war-weary souls
struggled to survive the frigid winter.

When we arrived at a battered school to host a shoebox distribution, we were escorted to a classroom filled with children waiting

patiently for what they had been promised; shoebox gifts. The windows in the school had been blown out and the children shivered from bone-chilling temperatures.

When the gifts were passed out, I'm sure the excitement created a little warmth for them, but my eye caught a boy sitting at a desk. He was the only child that didn't have a coat on—not even a jacket or sweater. His body was quivering and his lips were blue. For some reason, he wasn't enjoying the moment like the others. He examined the box, lifting the lid slightly and then putting it back down.

Puzzled, I walked over to check it out. At first glance, the box did not appear to have any toys, or anything else that would excite a kid—that is, until I pulled a T-shirt off the top. Underneath was a fleece-lined leather bomber jacket. The boy's eyes doubled in size as I shook it out, unbuttoned the jacket, and helped him put it on—a perfect fit!

Every class in the little school had been given shoeboxes that day, but in this one room, the only boy without a coat was given a box with a coat. Why wasn't that box given to the boy next to him who had a jacket? We don't know what's in these boxes; there is no way we can orchestrate something like this.

But God can.

These boxes had been packed by German Christians, and sent from our office in Berlin. I believe that a family in Germany had been touched by God to put a leather jacket in that shoebox.

Why?

For a little boy in Kosovo.

It was a direct result of the prayers of God's people and a demonstration of the warmth that the love of Jesus Christ sheds abroad.

I couldn't get that little boy off my mind as I traveled home, but I took comfort in knowing that he had felt the love of people who cared about him and prayed that through the simple gift of a shoebox and the Christmas story, that he would come to know the warmth of God's great love.

My hope and prayer for the coming year was that we could find ways to increase our ability to reach more kids with the Gospel. As the calendar rolled from December 31, 1998 to January 1, 1999, we knew we were in for a significant time in history—facing the end of a year, the end of a decade, and the end of a century—but the beginning of a new millennium. And our journey to bring the Gospel to unreached souls continues.

One Journey, Many Souls

S ome have never had the opportunity to walk through Africa's famine-stricken refugee camps, Asia's killing fields and tsunami-destroyed villages, Europe's war zones, drought regions of Oceania, or South American towns demolished by earthquakes.

But if you were able to see what I have witnessed, you would see "stick" people with only a layer of thin skin covering razor-thin bones due to malnourishment, the homeless wandering aimlessly looking for refuge, people crippled and blinded because of gunfire and shrapnel. You would see families craving just a drop of water as they gaze at their rice paddies burned up, reduced to chaff for the wind due to drought, or bodies buried under rubble, brick, and mortar. You would see children roaming the land fearfully and hear the young whimpering from hunger but not finding nourishment. You would witness the elderly left to somehow survive alone and hear wailing because of untreated disease and needless murder.

Not everyone can "go" abroad and give a cup of cold water in the name of Jesus (Matt. 10:42), or embrace the lonely and tell them of God's comfort, or rig up shelters from the storms of life. But everyone can do their part if only by supporting those who can and will "go." If you ask Him to make you aware, you may just find that you don't have to "go" any farther than next door or across the street to give the hope that Christ offers to someone in need. The Bible says, "Blessed is he who considers the poor" (Ps. 41:1).

The late Dr. Bob Pierce used to say, "I can't help everybody, but I can help some." We thank God for those who are touched with the compassion of Christ, making it possible for others to "go" and serve in His name; to carry immediate help and bring the light of God's spoken word to those who cannot distinguish light from darkness.

God has said, "Incline your ear, and come to Me. Hear, and your soul shall live" (Isa. 55:3).

Jesus brought comfort to souls and said, "Come to Me, all you who labor and are heavy laden, and I will give you rest" (Matt. 11:28).

Our bodies are the houses for the soul. Doctors can probe with X-ray but will never find the soul. Nevertheless, we carry within us the soul that was implanted by God, who fashioned us in His likeness.

Children love the time in school known as "show and tell." They learn to bring something they value and tell their classmates why the item is so special. The idea is to encourage kids to tell what they've learned about the things that mean the most to them. Life is a continual school room; what we learn, we pass on to others.

For Christians, our Teacher has given us the opportunity to "go and tell." The Bible says that "eternity is in the heart of man" (Eccles. 3:11), but we must speak God's truth to those who do not know the name of Jesus. The journey of one single shoebox has the potential of reaching many souls. So the next time you reach up for a shoebox, consider its potential of sprouting wings.

Birthday Parties for Shoebox Kids

Jonah dreamed of what it would be like to travel somewhere in the world and deliver shoeboxes to kids, but it wasn't possible. When he was just thirteen months old, he had been diagnosed with a brain tumor and spent years in and out of St. Jude Children's Hospital. When Jonah's parents asked him what he wanted for his eleventh birthday, he said he wanted to pack boxes for kids. This was something he could do.

Another young boy named Tomas, ten years old, had been battling a brain stem tumor for nearly two years. The Make-A-Wish Foundation contacted me with a request; Tomas wanted to come and see me—and he did. His dad, a policeman, accompanied him and told me how much Tomas loved Operation Christmas Child. Tomas had been packing shoeboxes for years. For his birthday party, he requested that his friends bring shoeboxes for needy children instead of presents for him.

People sometimes wonder if these gifts given with such love really get to those who need them. We received a letter about two boys in a cancer ward in Manila, Philippines, where a distribution took place. One boy had his right leg amputated. The team was sad because when he opened his box it contained a pair of shoes. They prayed and asked the Lord to please help the boy deal with the realization that he would never again wear a "pair" of shoes.

When they learned the boy in the next bed had his left leg amputated, they cringed as he opened his box. He pulled out a pair of socks. The moment was tense for those watching. Then the boys began to laugh. These two brave souls traded one sock for one shoe, and together they found humor and satisfaction in seeing their individual needs met.

We may not see the purpose in something, but God had overseen the delivery of two boxes that were just right for these boys who needed a glimmer of hope, a bond of friendship, and a lesson in finding joy.

Veronica's Army

Children in the West don't normally deal with life and death situations like kids around the world who live in war zones or experience great famines. But I am amazed to see the bravery demonstrated by children who deal with life and death matters when it comes to catastrophic diseases.

One young girl stands out in my mind—eleven-year-old Veronica Pomeroy who had cystic fibrosis. This grim lung disease didn't stop her from sharing the joy of Christmas with children she felt were much worse off than she.

When OCC was just getting started, Veronica latched on to the idea of kids helping kids. With classmates from her school in California, Veronica collected nearly three hundred gift-filled shoe-boxes the first year, eventually working up to 4,351. When I asked her to join our team going to Mexico City and help distribute these shoeboxes, she quickly accepted. That December, she and her mother headed to the poverty-stricken barrios of one of the world's largest cities.

Mexico City's thin air and heavy pollution took its toll on Veronica. She struggled to breathe, coughing frequently. Still she pressed on. After several stops to hand out gifts, she came to a garbage dump on the city's outskirts, a slum optimistically named *Bello Horizonte*, "Beautiful Horizon."

There among the mountains of trash, Veronica distributed tokens of Jesus' love to children ignored or forgotten by the outside world. "I guess it's a dream come true for them," Veronica said, "because it's probably their only gift."

While in Mexico, Veronica befriended seven-year-old Angelita Rodriguez and gave her the shoebox she had packed. The two girls sat down on a piece of cardboard and unpacked the box as Veronica explained each item; Angelita smiled and nodded sweetly. Veronica smiled too because her dream had come true; to pack a shoebox and put it in the hands of a new friend she hoped to see in Heaven someday.

DEAR GOD, IT'S ME

S hoeboxes are like snowflakes—no one is exactly the same. This is the case with our volunteers; I have never met two alike. One mother wanted her children to experience what the shoebox ministry was like "behind the scenes," and showed up at the warehouse one day with her two boys, ages thirteen and twenty-two. She wrote,

> The OCC staff graciously allowed us to help. We went through a training session and were then given an assignment to presort the shoeboxes.
>
> My twenty-two-year-old son, Reid, handed me and my other son boxes to check. Reid, while an adult, has the mental capacity of a three year old. He is autistic and has severe epilepsy. We had been teaching him about prayer and he began feeling confident enough to talk to the Lord.
>
> I challenged Reid to pray over the box he was holding, and he said, "Dear God, it's me, Reid. I pray for this boy, age five to seven. You know his name. I pray he loves his shoebox . . ." Then he opened his eyes and lifted the lid off the box and continued, "and the teddy bear and crayons. Keep him safe from the bad guys and make him strong and God, I pray he loves You . . . in the name of Jesus."

To all who were in earshot, it seemed a holy moment, and when Reid finished, there wasn't a dry eye in the place.

Families love doing shoeboxes together and it prompted us to implement Family Day, giving them a chance to work behind the scenes and provide a way for parents to introduce their children to helping others.

On these designated days, our staff walk kids through how to sort and inspect shoeboxes, and about programs like "Build a Box Online." But most important, they learn through interactive training sessions the results of getting shoeboxes to kids living in difficult parts of the world. They are also given a taste of going through *The Greatest Journey*, and for many, this is their first step in learning to do for others.

"Breaking in" a Box

S hoebox gifts reflect the givers. Often boxes have a theme like sports or craft items. Along with hygiene items and school supplies, most boxes will have some type of music; harmonicas, CDs, musical stuffed animals, or dolls, trucks, and balls. But one thing they all have in common—they are given in love.

It's hard to fathom what life would be never having received a gift from anybody. Many don't believe this is possible, but we've witnessed children's perplexity when they are handed a shoebox. They don't know what they're supposed to do. One little boy shook his box and concluded something was inside. But the lid was taped to the box. So after studying the matter, he took a stick and bore a hole through the top large enough that he could poke his hand through it and pull the toys out. He became silent, having no words adequate to express his delight. You can imagine how puzzled he was when he discovered the lid lifted off.

Children of the Tepihuan Indians, who live in the mountain regions of Durango, Mexico, had never seen a gift, much less received one. This was a perfect destination for Operation Christmas Child, because when there is no concept of giving, there is no concept of Jesus Christ.

The team did the distribution and stared with wonder as the children stood in silence, not knowing what to do. When the team grasped the situation, they quickly integrated among the children and gave them a spontaneous lesson in shoebox opening. They even had to show the children what to do with the toys inside. When they heard music boxes humming and harmonicas playing, they were mesmerized and thought the boxes themselves played music.

Most endearing, though, was to watch their faces as the Christmas story was presented. This was the first time they had heard the name of Jesus. God's Word and God's love turned this little town inside out. As hearts responded, music filled the air.

NOT A LOT OF MONEY, JUST A LITTLE BIT OF LOVE

Kids naturally respond to someone who cares. Show a little interest in them and they generally come to life. A wonderful surprise has been to see how Operation Christmas Child is a teaching tool to children who pack the boxes.

A mom and dad were listening to their kids as they were driving home from church one Sunday. They had heard a presentation I had made about OCC and wanted to help.

As the mother related the story she said,

"We thought it was a good idea to give them money and drop them off at the store to buy their gifts. But we also thought about the stories we had heard—that the project not only provides for needy children but also teaches the children who pack the boxes about giving sacrificially. The church had been told to 'pray for what goes in the boxes and pray for the children who would receive them.' Wow! If we give the children the money, they may miss an important lesson."

"How serious are you about wanting to light up the world with shoeboxes for kids?" she asked her children. 'We really want to do this Mom, will you help us? Mr. Graham said it wouldn't cost a lot of money, just a little love,' the children answered. It was their way of asking for a little bit of money."

Hmmm, I thought. "Well, do you have enough love to empty your piggy banks?"

Silence.

"I turned around and watched their faces fall. "We thought you would give us some money to buy the presents," they shot back.

"Before I could react, my husband who had stayed out of the conversation said, 'Here's what we'll do. Your mom and I will give you each seven dollars for the cost of sending the boxes to Mr. Graham so that he can deliver them for you. But you'll have to pay for what goes in the boxes'."

"There was a painfully long silence."

"When we arrived home, the kids piled out of the car in a hush. My husband and I were disappointed that their 'little bit of love' was short-lived."

"As I prepared dinner, I questioned myself as to whether we should have made it easy for them to be givers. When I called the family to the table, my husband and I suddenly fell silent. All four of our children walked into the kitchen holding empty shoeboxes they had found, and inside the boxes they had each emptied their piggy banks. With smiles they asked, 'After we eat can we go and buy our presents?'"

"While our children enjoyed spaghetti and meatballs, my husband and I ate crow. We had not exhibited much faith in our children, but they exhibited an enormous amount of selfless love."

"My husband and I walked behind our children through the aisles of the neighborhood store that afternoon and watched them carefully make their selections. When we approached the check-out, my husband rounded the corner and held up four items. 'Hey kids,' he said, 'thought you might want to light up those boxes. This is my contribution to show how proud we are of you for loving others so generously.' He handed them four flashlights, batteries and all."

"The moral of the story is that our kids give us lots of experiences that require a lot of learning on our part. The Lord 'enlightens' us every day and in so many ways. He is the Light of the World."

Many pastors and parents have told us that OCC has helped to foster a love for missions within the hearts of children. Parents thank me for giving them an opportunity to teach their child how to give. This is important. If children learn to give today, they will likely always be givers. Raising another generation to give generously to ministry work is essential in obedience to God. The shoebox ministry gives children a hands-on way to serve the Lord at very young ages, and has been proven to bless them as much as their gifts bless children around the world who need to know Him as Lord.

The Knock on a Neighbor's Door

Many people do not become givers because they've never been exposed to the idea. And as our culture changes and becomes more "me" centered, we sometimes fail to recognize opportunities that come knocking.

One of our faithful shoebox packers made her motto "neighbors helping neighbors," and she put it to work in her OCC endeavors.

"I had never known my neighbor," she said. "We both stayed very busy taking care of our families. I had always been hesitant to answer the door to unexpected visitors because generally they wanted me to get involved in community affairs or give money to neighborhood drives. But my life would not be as rich today had I ignored the knock on my door—the day I officially met my neighbor who asked me this simple question:

'Will you donate a shoebox for a good cause?' Just a shoebox? That's not too much to ask. I quickly invited her in and went back into the closet and found the best shoebox that still had a matching lid. I proudly handed it to her and she thanked me so sweetly and then said, 'I'm so sorry, I didn't communicate very well; I was asking if you would fill a shoebox with toys for a child.'"

"She then proceeded to explain Operation Christmas Child. After hearing some of her stories and watching her eyes fill with tears, I just couldn't turn down her further request to take the box back, fill it up with toys, wrap some paper around it and drop it off at her church. Still not too much to ask, so I agreed."

"When I arrived the next week at the church, I had one of my children run the box into the office. But when my daughter came back to the car she said, 'Mom, you gotta come in here and see this!'"

"My imagination raced. Nervously, I jumped out of the car believing that she had seen something unexplainable. She had, indeed. We followed the church secretary down the hallway into the fellowship center where boxes—too many to count—were stacked along three walls. Aisles had been organized and the place was humming with activity."

"I don't know what took me by surprise the most—the number of boxes, the array of color, or the adults and children busying about. Maybe it was that our one little box seemed to lose its glory in the shadow of such generosity. I gulped as my daughter looked up at me, knowing that I had bragged all the way there about what a wonderful job I had done at putting this box together."

"The secretary thanked me for the box and then put her hands on it and prayed, 'Lord, thank you for the hands that packed this box. Thank you for the prayers that will send it on its way. We don't know where it will end up, but You do. We may never know, but You will. We pray that the gifts will bring joy but more important, we pray that the message the box carries will touch the sad heart of one so small and win a soul to Your kingdom. Amen.'"

"By now, I was crying. When my daughter looked up and saw the tears, she began to cry. The knock on my front door changed my life and my family's life. We ended up collecting boxes from others we knew and even volunteered to help at the church. (Did I mention that we started going to church?) My neighbor and I have become like sisters and her church family has become ours."

"My one little box returned a great dividend when we learned that it had traveled all the way to Southeast Asia and found its way into the hands of a little girl whose eyes were blind. It opened up the window of my soul and I pray it will do the same for her—that Jesus will bring the light of salvation into her heart. I can tell you that when someone knocks at my door, I open it; otherwise, I may miss a blessing from Heaven".

"Knock and the door will be open to you" (Matt. 7:7 NIV).

I Got Lots of Smiles

I f that brings a smile, consider a seven-year-old girl named Gaukhar who received a shoebox. She was at the edge of a distribution site in Central Asia. Gaukhar had enthusiastically received her box, but soon discovered that there were not enough boxes to go around. Many left sad.

Gaukhar's father asked that she give her baby brother a toy for his very own out of her shoebox. She sweetly complied. As a young mother nearby observed, she approached Gaukhar and asked if she would share a toy with her little one too. She looked sheepishly into her box and over at the child, then lifted out something that would please him. The idea caught on as others came asking for something too, until Gaukhar's box was nearly depleted.

When she arrived home, her mother said, "What did you get, Gaukhar?" She hugged her mother and said, "Lots of smiles—and this pretty shoebox!" And she raised the nearly empty box to show her mother. I'm quite sure she had to choke back some emotion; but her heart must have overflowed with satisfaction knowing that her daughter had learned that there is great joy in giving and giving and giving.

An empty shoebox wrapped in happiness is a gift all by itself. Story after story tells of joys the colorful boxes bring to children who have little to nothing. Many of these children keep their boxes for years, boxes that endure extreme heat, tape that turns yellow, cardboard that absorbs humidity; but for many, just to have their very own box is a treasure chest to them and something they can call their very own.

THE POWER OF THE LETTER

S addam Hussein was still in power in Iraq when Sami Dagher called me. He wanted to take shoeboxes to the Christians in Baghdad who were oppressed and discouraged. It was after the first Gulf War. Sami is a powerful example of using shoebox gifts to open up doors—and an example of Samaritan's Purse working through local pastors and churches—through people who understand the culture, know the lay of the land, and can speak the language. Shoeboxes in the hands of our national church partners are keys to this children's ministry.

Sami had been in and out of Iraq for years and had been praying for an opportunity to start a church in the city, but the door always slammed shut.

Samaritan's Purse sent the boxes Sami requested. He was so excited to see how God would work, and completed all the necessary steps to get the boxes into the country. But when Sami arrived, he was told that he could not distribute them.

Instead, they were confiscated by Hussein's regime and given to the Iraqi people on Saddam Hussein's birthday, in the dictator's name. Sami was discouraged until he began hearing stories from people who had received the gifts; boxes with Bibles, Christian literature, letters and pictures from the senders.

A couple of months after the distribution, we received a call from someone in the States who had received a letter from an Iraqi family thanking them for the gift and asking for help. Their daughter had a blood disease and needed medicine impossible to get in Iraq due to embargoes and United Nations sanctions. Without it, however, the child would die. The family who received the request didn't know how to reply, so they wrote to Samaritan's Purse.

The day we received the letter, we tracked Sami down to get his advice and learned that he was on his way to Iraq. "I am going there now," Sami said with excitement, "and I can get the medicine here in Jordan and take it to the family in Iraq." Within a week of us receiving the letter, Sami delivered the medicine in the name of Jesus, placing it in the father's hands.

The family could not believe it—they were shocked. They were so moved and said, "Christians are the only ones who care." Because of one simple gift—in the name of Jesus Christ—the entire family came to salvation.

The family that packed the box and made the extra effort to send a letter, with a return address, never dreamed their generosity would result in an entire family coming to Christ. These are the spiritual dividends of a simple gift.

Saddaam Hussein had given what was not his to give—but God had a plan. Instead of the boxes going to Christians who already knew the Lord, He used an unlikely man to place the boxes into the hands of those who needed to know that Christians are the ones who care, because Jesus Christ is the One who comforts and saves. "We love Him because He first loved us" (1 John 4:19).

Escape to Safety

A letter found in a shoebox means a great deal to the recipient. A woman called our office and told how her family and church had packed and sent boxes not knowing where they would go. Letters were included, asking the recipients to write back. The daughter kept a candle in the window in remembrance to pray for these children. Many months after, the daughter received a letter from Bosnia, but was unable to translate it.

A couple had spoken at their church a few weeks before and told of their escape from Bosnia. As they fled their home, they turned to look back and saw their house blown up. Under God's hand of protection, they managed to leave the country and found refuge with many other families until they could find their way to America. They had not been able to contact any family that had been left behind and had no way to know if they were dead or alive. They requested that the church pray that word would come to them.

The family managed to locate the couple from Bosnia who translated the letter. Not only was the daughter's heart moved to hear the message written by the shoebox recipient, but as the Bosnian couple translated the note, they discovered it was a letter from her cousin's daughter. What seemed to be two different prayers were answered in one letter because of one shoebox.

This illustrates so clearly a story from Monica Anderson, regional area coordinator for us in central Indiana.

"We have packed many boxes over the years, but when my son William packed his boxes at the age of ten, he spent a great deal of time planning and preparing each step and each item and then brought them to me for inspection. 'Look Mom,' he said, 'the boys who get these boxes are going to be excited to see all the neat things inside.'"

"I didn't want to deflate him, but I immediately noticed that he had not included letters. When I questioned him he said, 'There's so much in these boxes they'll never miss the letters!' I saw this as a teachable moment and said, 'William, most of these kids have never received a letter in their lives. Those who get them treasure them. Often the letter means more than the toys. The letter is a way to explain why you've sent the gift. It is a way to convey God's love for them and that Jesus is the greatest gift of all.'"

"With those few words of admonition, William returned to his desk to write his letters and slip them into the boxes along with his school picture. The boxes were sent off, wrapped in prayer."

"Five months later, William was the recipient of two letters. One from three year old Victor, whose father had helped him write a thank-you note and sent a picture from their home in Jinja, Uganda. The second letter was from Mwesigwa, age eleven, from Kampala who also sent a picture of himself, with each corner of the photo dog-eared and yellowed."

"When William realized that people from these regions of Uganda did not have very reliable postal service, he knew that these letters were gifts from the Lord; a confirmation that his gifts had been received and the message of God's love had gotten through. We may never know the full impact it will make in these young boys but one thing for sure, Jesus has been made known."

We love stories about moms, because the Bible commends mothers who nurture their children in God's Word. The apostle Paul wrote that he wanted young Timothy to travel with him on his missionary journeys (Acts 16:3) and why.

"When I call to remembrance the genuine faith that is in you, which dwelt first in your grandmother Lois and your mother Eunice, and I am persuaded is in you also" (2 Tim. 1:5).

Timothy's father was not a believer, yet Timothy was raised to love and serve the Lord. This should be a great encouragement to mothers.

THE SHOEBOX WITH WINGS CAUSE A FLUTTER

Children whose mothers reject them are left with enduring pain. God has used Operation Christmas Child to bring them rays of hope through gifts of smiles and laughter that colors a rather dark world.

Most Westerners would find it difficult to even imagine living in an orphanage. Orphans in North America are largely absorbed through foster-care programs. But in developing countries and nations at war, orphanages exist; many overflow. Children and teenagers long to know the warmth of home, but many who enter orphanages do not leave until they become of age, then they are turned out into a lonesome and frightening world. So when we hear stories about those who are transplanted into Christian homes and given the opportunity to become "someone's child," our hearts flutter with joy. We found such a child from Russia and heard what happened when she recognized the infamous flying shoebox.

Elena and her sister had a troubled home. The girls slept on beds with no linens and little food, while their mom and dad drank and left them home alone much of the time. Eventually, the girls were placed in an orphanage where Elena, at eight years old, finally had the chance to go to school. While her memories of the orphanage were not always good, she loves to remember the announcement that was made one day. A party was coming and each child would receive a gift. A gift? She couldn't imagine who would bring gifts to unknowns. But excitement mounted.

Elena related the story in broken English with eyes that spoke as strongly as her words.

I'll never forget walking into the room and seeing boxes piled up. There was a puppet show, a story, some singing, and then every child was given a box wrapped in the prettiest paper. I had never received a gift that was wrapped. It made me feel special.

I don't remember every item that was in my box that day, but I do remember three special things. One was the bright wrapping paper. That was a gift in itself. We didn't have places to keep our few possessions and I clung to this box and admired its beauty. The orphanage was dismal. Our uniforms were grey and dingy. The sun didn't shine much in Russia and my world was dark and uninteresting. But to see the bright colors made my heart feel happy. One of the gifts was a toothbrush and toothpaste. That night when I squeezed the tube and saw the pretty colors ooze out it made me smile; it tasted so good and gave me a clean feeling. To top it off, I received the booklet, *The Greatest Gift of All* in my own language. I began to understand the significance of a gift and what God had done for us when He gave the gift of His Son, when we didn't even know Him.

Today, Elena and her sister live in the United States. Kris and Sarah Hagemeier reached out with God's love and adopted the sisters and have raised them in a Christian home. Just how did this happen? In Elena's words,

There was a contest at the orphanage. My sister and I won scholarships to a summer camp in Missouri and left for America. The three-week camp was held at a church and we got to know an associate pastor and his wife and two young sons. My sister and I started thinking of them as our little brothers and wondered what it would be like to be part of a family.

After returning to Russia, we received a letter from the Hagemeirs asking if we would like for them to adopt us. We had no way of answering back, but things began happening and we were excited to think of going back to America.

Six months later they came to Russia. They told us how the Lord had given them peace that this was the thing to do. They asked their boys, ages three and five, if they would like us to be their sisters and suggested they think about it. The next morning, the boys ran into their parents' room, jumped up on the bed and said, "We should adopt the girls."

We moved to the United States and inherited a wonderful family who has taken us to church and taught us God's truth. One Sunday my Dad was giving the announcements and showed the OCC video. When the logo appeared on the screen and I saw the boxes, I turned to my mom and squealed "I got one of those. I remember the flying shoebox." I remembered the bright colors making me so happy."

My Dad told me that they packed shoeboxes for OCC and said that my sister and I could do it too. Becoming part of OCC on the giving end was more happiness than I could imagine. On top of that, I was selected as one of nineteen kids to go on a distribution to hand out shoeboxes. It was *déjà vu*. I relived my experience of getting one of these incredible gifts that made a profound impact on my life, and OCC has given me the chance to share what Jesus has done for me.

Elena told us later about her experience at the orphanage.

It was not a religious orphanage, but from time to time a priest visited and spoke to the children. What he told us interested me. Each child was given a cross on a chain. He told us that if we would always keep it, we would go to Heaven. But he warned that if we lost it, we would not be allowed into Heaven. Some who lost it didn't seem upset, but at night I would pray never to lose it.

But one day the cross went missing. Frightened to think of being shut out of Heaven, fear haunted me. But when I came to the United States and heard the whole story about the cross of Jesus and what He did for me, I confessed my sins to Him. The revelation that He is not on the cross but in my heart to stay is what makes the difference. Salvation in Christ is not gained by hanging a cross around my neck, but allowing His sacrifice to "cross out" my sin and give me a new heart.

Elena has been a joy to our Samaritan's Purse family and OCC team. She says, *"spasibo"* (thank you). The Lord has put in her heart a love for others and is seeking Him about future service, possibly in Asia. She is studying missions at Ozark Christian College and hopes to learn Mandarin so that she can one day communicate the Gospel message to those in a land that is not her home.

Only God knows what else He has in store for this young lady who found hope for the future—in a box that colored her world with happiness.

COLORED BY A RAINBOW

Personalities of shoebox packers are often reflected in the contents of a shoebox, adding splashes of sweetness and sometimes humor. One little boy packed his box and wrote, "I love to climb trees. My dad calls me a little monkey, so I'm sending you a stuffed monkey. Press his belly and he'll chatter away." He ended the letter by saying, "God created all the animals and told us to take care of them, and God takes care of us."

I've always encouraged packers to include a key toy—a doll for a girl, a truck for a boy, a stuffed animal that's easy to cuddle, or a ball. That "key toy" is usually latched onto and treasured. But it is always fun to hear stories about why and how people pack their boxes. If a girl enjoys play jewelry, she'll often pack some in her box. If a boy enjoys sports, he'll find a way to squeeze some kind of ball in with other things. If adults pack boxes, they'll often pack things similar to what they enjoyed when they were children.

So it wouldn't be far-fetched to imagine someone who enjoys art to pack a box like Lesky received. This young boy is the son of a farmer who lives on a small East Indonesian island. Lesky loves to draw and color, but art supplies are an expensive commodity in the remote city near South Timor where our OCC partners did a shoebox distribution at a local church.

Lesky would have been grateful for anything inside the box, but when he pulled out a full set of drawing pencils in every color imaginable, he believed that God had granted him favor. His little world that day was colored by a rainbow.

"Truly, what the Lord has been doing through OCC boxes is beyond our imagination," an Indonesian pastor wrote. "God's powerful love compels us to reach out to these children. Prayers that go with the boxes have broken through impenetrable barriers, hostilities, hatreds, and fundamentalism. Those we minister to have seen our service to them in the name of Jesus Christ, resulting many times in reconciliation. This is really amazing. Please keep working with us for Indonesia, through whatever difficulties and challenges may arise, to see hearts transformed in my country."

We often take for granted the simple things in life. So next time you see a rainbow in the sky, thank God for coloring our world with His promises, His fragrance of love, and the seeds of faith that lighten hearts.

Sounds of the Season

Trash heaps that dot third world countries are not just places for refuse, they are home to many; and for children, the garbage dumps are their playgrounds. They need something to brighten their lives. Samaritan's Purse is in the Christmas spirit year-round, looking for ways to reach these children.

Salvation Army hand bells ring at store entrances. Christmas music plays through speaker systems in restaurants. These are the sounds of the season in Western countries.

But while kids may be kids, life is different for many who live in places like Nicaragua. The kids there are probably a little dirtier than ours, but their hearts are no different. Some are tender, some are hostile, and all have the potential of coming to know the Christmas Child. They are the reason for the season. To watch these kids open packages and hear their laughter—and hear their "thank-yous,"—this is the sound of Christmas ringing in our ears.

Reality is, however, that when children without daily meals, without family, and without love never have the opportunity to hear about Jesus, the sounds of every season for them ring with hopelessness.

This is a description of many desperate families who scavenge for food in trash heaps outside the capital city of Managua. We renovated a school some years ago in La Chureca.

The LaChureca Dump was transformed into a Heap of Happiness when the scavenging children saw our trucks rolling toward them— trucks not filled with more garbage, but trucks filled with shoebox gifts; one for each child, staring in wondrous hope for a surprise that had the potential of lifting them out of despair and into God's promise for a better tomorrow.

So it was really no surprise to hear little ten-year-old Francisca Castillo, affectionately known as "Coco," say, "It's very beautiful." Those were her soft-spoken words as she peered into her shoebox of toys.

The shoeboxes were also instrumental in staging the largest evangelistic children's rally ever held in the capital city of Managua. Following a massive distribution throughout the city by twelve hundred local churches, more than one hundred and fifty-five thousand children came to hear a Gospel presentation sponsored by the Billy Graham Evangelistic Association.

Many of the children clutched their new toys as they listened carefully to a colorful stage character named Miguel talk about God's special gift to them—His Son, Jesus Christ. More than twenty-one thousand children responded at the time of invitation, giving Christians the opportunity to talk and pray with the children.

This is where the follow-up ministry of OCC becomes so critical. Long before the day of such a rally, our ministries have prepared local churches to train their members in evangelism and discipleship "after the shoebox." OCC is training pastors and teachers to invest in these children who will one day be parents, pastors, and church leaders. This is the hope for their future and for the continuation of the effective ministry of the church.

I have worked in Nicaragua since the civil war between the Sandanistas and the Contras. Samaritan's Purse actually trained a chaplain corps for the Contra army. What a thrill it is to return and meet many of these men who have been called into the ministry and are pastors of some of the strongest evangelical churches in these countries. Many now serve as partners with Operation Christmas Child. God's work is full circle, and He completes what He starts in the hearts of those who serve Him.

A Ball Got the Church Rolling

Meet Bismarck. When he was ten years old, this Nicaraguan boy received a brightly wrapped shoebox at an Operation Christmas Child party. He was ecstatic with this gift, but he never imagined the effect it would have on the rest of his life.

Reflecting on that day, years later, Bismarck recalled his excitement over that box, including what became his most prized possession—a soccer ball. The pastor who gave him the shoebox impacted him so greatly that Bismarck began attending Sunday school and asked Jesus into his heart. At age thirteen, he felt that God wanted him to study the Bible more and eventually managed to get into Bible school.

As his faith grew, God placed a strong desire in his heart to reach out to children in his community, just as his pastor had reached out to him.

Bismarck began holding little meetings in the same community he had grown up in, reading Bible stories and teaching the children songs, starting with five kids all from the same family. He used the soccer ball he had received in his shoebox years before to reach out to the gangs in the area and many came to Christ. In less than a year, the number had grown to sixty.

Parents began to take notice of what was happening and started attending the sessions. In time, this little Bible study group became Siloe Church where Bismarck serves as the youth pastor.

We have always marveled at the works of God and we are constantly amazed to see how "shoebox kids" grow up using what has been put in their hands to testify about what the Lord has done for them. Whether it's a flashlight to shine the light of God's Word or a ball to get the church rolling, God will bless in everything you put your hand to when it is done for His glory (Deut. 15:10).

A Shoebox—A Tool in God's Hand

"What's in your hand that God can use?" David Ruiz asked this question to several people sitting around a table one day. He challenged them to consider a simple shoebox.

David has worked many years with BGEA and has translated for me when I've preached crusades and festivals throughout Mexico and Central and South America. David has also served with our OCC team for many years helping to blaze new trails in this strategic part of the world. He has met many people who were saved at one of my father's crusades; others who were saved during our festivals. But David told me what an impact the shoeboxes have had on younger generations; kids who may have never had the chance to attend such a meeting. Instead, they learned of Jesus Christ because of a shoebox.

"The shoebox is a tool for the Gospel," David said. "I think of a pastor in Guladajara, Mexico, who had a heart for the poor children. His church had an orphanage that cared for these children, but it wasn't until OCC came that he had a tool for evangelism to reach others outside his church. Some of the children from that orphanage are now grown and trained to teach the Bible course made available by Samaritan's Purse. Others are Sunday school teachers and pastors. That generation is now teaching the next generation."

"I can recall one pastor from Peru trying many ways to reach people for Christ. Nothing worked. He felt frustrated and was ready to leave the ministry. 'There is no response here,' he said. Then OCC came to his small town and children were invited to his church. Soon the parents began coming. The pastor's ministry changed, the church changed, and the community changed."

The OCC team motivates pastors and churches to teach their people to reach out to their neighbors, friends, and family with the Gospel. We come alongside existing evangelical ministries already established in these countries mobilizing the Christian community to work together to put the shoeboxes into the hands of the children. This is perpetuated from one generation to another. We thank God that He has empowered their service as they are obedient to His mission.

Moldova 2005: Candy is a rare treat in places like this rural village in Moldova. When children open their boxes, the first items they often reach for are the lollipops and peppermints.

Panama 2007: Many children will never receive a high school or college diploma. To receive a certificate commending children for completing a 12-lesson Bible study brings a sense of accomplishment.

Cambodia 2007: Receiving a Christmas present for the first time in her life brought great joy to this young Cambodian girl.

Mali 2007: Little Harry from Washington, DC, hoped his gift and letter would travel far. He never dreamed it would go all the way to this little boy in Timbuktu.

Colombia 2007: Children love the excitement of the shoebox gifts, but children treasure the Word of God found in the colorful Gospel booklet and love to learn about Jesus.

China 2007: "The box is like a seed," said a Chinese Christian who works with OCC. "The children learn the meaning of Christmas."

Philippines 2008: It doesn't get too primitive for OCC. These children listen intently to the story of God's Gift to the world—Jesus—as they prepare to receive gifts from Christians.

Bolivia 2008: Farming families in Bolivia struggle to earn a living. Parents cannot afford to buy Christmas presents. The special delivery of shoeboxes was a memorable event for these children at Christmas.

Zimbabwe 2008: Exotic forms of transportation are sometimes used to deliver gifts to isolated corners of the world.

Macedonia 2008: In this slum settlement, children live among heaps of garbage in dilapidated shacks. Shoebox gifts brought rays of hope to the forlorn landscape as children heard the Christmas story.

UK 2008: Her Royal Highness Princess Anne (of the United Kingdom) paid tribute to OCC when she visited our warehouse in Weston-super-Mare.

Cameroon 2009: Pygmy children from the Baka tribe received stuffed animals to cuddle.

2009: Volunteering in an OCC processing center is fun and rewarding. There's plenty to do and plenty to smile about.

India 2009: Ox cart, bicycle, and by foot are everyday transportation in this India village.

2009: Several Minnesota Vikings' players helped children pack shoeboxes for kids around the world.

Sudan 2010: Happy children enjoy their gift boxes and the thrill of looking forward to starting *The Greatest Journey* discipleship program offered through local churches.

Romania 2010: Taking a Peek: The sense of anticipation is too much for these little girls who couldn't wait to see what treasures were hidden in the box.

Haiti 2010: Former Governor Sarah Palin traveled to Haiti with some family members to take part in the Samaritan's Purse OCC shoebox distribution following the earthquake.

Haiti 2011: Caring for Orphans: Greta Van Susteren hands out shoebox gifts to children at an orphanage that was destroyed by the 2010 earthquake. The orphanage was rebuilt by Samaritan's Purse and named "The Greta Home" in honor of her efforts to help the Haitian people.

North Carolina 2011: Bikers with Boxes: Motorcycles roared through the gates of the Billy Graham Library in Charlotte to deliver hundreds of shoeboxes.

Dominican Republic 2011: My daughter, Cissie Graham Lynch, enjoys explaining to a little boy about the toys in the box and the love of those who sent it.

Dominican Republic 2011: Sean Hannity, longtime supporter of Samaritan's Purse and fan of OCC, traveled with his family and me after Christmas to hand out shoeboxes. Sean's son Patrick on right.

Mongolia 2011: Long-haired yaks are used to transport OCC gifts to children living in remote villages in Mongolia's Gobi Desert.

Philippines 2011: Christmas joy in the streets.

USA 2012: If you packed 100 million shoeboxes into a 40-foot sea container—like this one specially decorated for OCC—you would need 13,000 tractor-trailer loads.

USA 2012: OCC volunteers don't mind standing in lines at Christmastime—OCC processing lines that is.

2012: Christian recording artist Matthew West at his concert contributes to the 100 millionth shoebox that spokesperson Evilyn Pinnow eventually hand-delivered to a little girl in Dominican Republic.

Dominican Republic 2012: Evilyn Pinnow delivers the 100 millionth shoebox to Brenda Valdez just before Christmas.

Ecuador 2012: I took my eldest grandchild, CJ Graham, on her first shoebox distribution. The children were overwhelmed by the gifts, excitement, and attention.

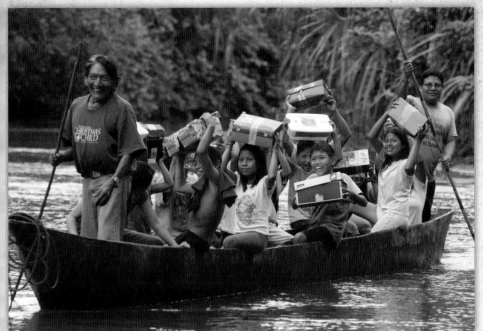

Ecuador 2012: Transformed by Christ: Decades ago, Mincaye Enquedi murdered American missionaries Nate Saint and Jim Elliott. Today, Mincaye is a Christian pastor who partners with OCC to share the Gospel with children in Ecuador.

Mexico 2013: Eleven-year-old Jorge Rodriguez reads through *The Greatest Journey* in Santiago Papasquiaro, Durango, in the trash heap.

Verna and Bill Pauls have traveled with me to do shoebox distributions around the world. They have been responsible for making OCC a huge success in their home state of Colorado. This photo is from the Pauls's 2012 Christmas Card.

Florida 2013: Celebrating 100 million shoeboxes at the Orange County Convention Center in Orlando, (left to right) Ricky Skaggs, Tommy Coomes, Mary Damron, Dennis Agajanian, and myself reminisce about the 1995 trip across Mount Igman before singing "God on the Mountain" for 10,000 guests and OCC staff and volunteers.

THE SHOEBOX OCTOPUS

I t was 1998. Lima, Peru was my destination; Operation Christmas
Child was already there.

A lot was happening in and around the sprawling capital city
sometimes called El Pulpo, meaning "the octopus." I was going to
preach four nights at the National Stadium. Glenn Alsworth, a good
friend of mine from Port Alsworth, Alaska, and a fellow pilot, flew to
North Carolina. I had really wanted him to go on this trip with me
because Glenn loves children. We were planning a huge children's
rally on Saturday morning. So we boarded the Samaritan's Purse
plane—the MU2—and headed south, making stops in Panama and
Ecuador, then following the South American coastline to Peru. Off
in the distance was the fifth largest city in Latin America—Lima—
overlooking the Pacific Ocean.

OCC had been busy—very busy—delivering seventy thousand
shoeboxes. Our church partners in Lima were prepared and ready to
see that every child who received a shoebox also received our Gospel
literature, along with an invitation to attend a Saturday morning
event. We expected twenty thousand kids. We also invited the parents to come and stay for the festival that night.

Because of the power of prayer and the power of a simple gift,
more than twenty thousand kids showed up—way more. We watched
as seventy thousand tried to get into the stadium that morning for
the children's rally. Before saying "praise the Lord" and "hallelujah,"
this could have been a disaster.

The temperature was hovering around one hundred degrees.
The rally was delayed several hours just trying to get all the people
inside. Fire trucks were brought in to spray the crowd with cool water

to prevent heatstroke. The swelling numbers and heat misery could have sparked a stampede, causing little children to be crushed. But by God's grace, the meeting finally got underway. The children were enthused with the Gospel program, and many thousands responded to the invitation to come to Jesus.

In a way, the shoebox distributions had become like the octopus—with its arms reaching into neighborhoods, towns, and villages. When an octopus wants to move fast it releases a jet of water that propels it forward. The tremendous amount of prayer that had gone into this massive distribution had propelled the invitation forward, sending more than a triple number of people to our evangelistic rally.

While in the city, we didn't want to forget the kids who were innocent victims of imprisonment, so we loaded up shoeboxes and went to a women's prison. Many young women at the time of incarceration are pregnant; their babies are born in the prison and are often allowed to stay with their mothers, which was certainly the case at this facility. Mothers could not believe we would bring gifts to their children. Their hearts became tender as they watched the joy on their children's faces and heard their laughter bouncing off the cinderblock walls. But like the octopus, the shoeboxes reached more than the children we were ministering to.

We met three young women—one an American citizen, the other two Russian. The American girl had been tricked by her boyfriend to carry a suitcase of drugs back into the country. She got caught. The Russian girls were in prison for drugs also.

Glenn Alsworth, who speaks Russian, began talking with the two girls. It was the first time in months that anyone had spoken to them in their language. It encouraged them and Glenn had their ear as he witnessed and shared the Gospel.

The father of the American girl was a tough Pennsylvania cop. When her story appeared on American television, he was interviewed and said he would not lift a finger to help his daughter. In fact, he said he wouldn't even cross the street to try and save her. But God touched his heart and he went to Peru to help win her freedom.

The purpose of our visit to the Peruvian prison that day was to deliver shoebox gifts to children, but in the process God led us to others who needed a touch from the Lord, and three young ladies that day found a reason for hope.

When one of the Russian girls was released and came to America sometime later, she called Glenn to thank him for what he had done for her.

Following the release of the American girl, she and her father appeared on television, both in tears, warning others about drug trafficking and the trap that imprisons unsuspecting travelers.

Shoeboxes do more than just put smiles on faces—they have the potential to bring hope and lasting joy.

"Now hope does not disappoint, because the love of God has been [shed abroad] in our hearts" (Rom. 5:5).

FEET THAT CARRY
GOOD NEWS

B e prepared [to preach the Word] in season and out of season . . .
with great patience and careful instruction" (2 Tim. 4:2 NIV). A
man who visited Vietnam put this into practice.

Visiting Southeast Asia he stopped along the street to get a shoeshine. This trade is a thing of the past in America, but in Vietnam
shoeshine stands line the streets, providing income for boys who
wait patiently for their next customer.

A teenage boy greeted the man with a smile and told him he
shines shoes to buy food for his family. After they visited, the man
paid the boy and invited him to a shoebox distribution at a local
church, and the boy showed up. This is an example of authentic
"street evangelism."

The teenager received a box containing a battery-powered cassette player and a variety of Christian music tapes. These aren't
everyday items for children in places like Vietnam. Not only did the
boy enjoy the player, but he shared it with twenty other guys his age
that lived in a boys' home. Their pastime became listening to the
music and learning English.

He was so thrilled that he returned to the church to say *"aw-
koon ch'ran"* (thank you) and was invited to participate in Bible and
English classes. He enrolled and faithfully attended, eventually finding salvation in Christ. He is now sharing with the other guys in
the home what God has done for him. The shoeshine boy became a
Christian and now has a shining testimony for the Lord.

This is why we believe God has blessed Operation Christmas
Child. The numbers of boxes collected are staggering, but hearts
changed is the reason for ministering to children. And as the century

drew to a close, we thanked God for His guidance and recommitted our resolve to watch Him do more as the clock ticked down to the stroke of midnight.

EXTINGUISHING THE DARKNESS

Midnight for Africa never seemed to give way to dawn. Civil wars continued to pit tribe against tribe, earning the nickname "the Dark Continent." Africa's children faced a bleak future. An AIDs epidemic was sweeping the continent. United Nations secretary general, Kofi Annan, said, "More people have died of AIDS in Africa than in all the wars on the continent."*

By 2000, twenty-four million Africans were infected with the virus. In the poorest parts of Africa, children born with HIV have a life expectancy of only five to ten years.

That was a fact of life for Emily, age nine. She was all too familiar with AIDS, having been infected the day she was born. She saw the terrible way the plague took her father and feared what would happen to her mother and herself.

But Christmas 2000 came to Emily in the form of a shoebox from an American girl who empathized with the Ugandan girl's plight. Lesley Clementi was also born HIV-positive. Like Emily, she was the only child infected in her family and asked, "Why me?"

Instead of feeling sorry for herself, Lesley poured her heart into her shoebox. Amid the cuddly bear, the hairbrush, the candy, and other gifts, she placed a note. "I want to let you know I care for you and I always will, no matter what happens in our lives. You're always going to have a friend. All you need in life is one . . . if you ever have a problem or fears, turn to Jesus and He will help you."

And we have seen this happen with thousands of children across Africa. We were told by a man who reached out to Emily, "Through these gifts, [the children] have seen the Lord."

Shoeboxes do carry light into the darkness because the Light of the world pierces the gloomy prospect of African's tomorrow. "The light shines through the darkness, and the darkness can never extinguish it" (John 1:5 NLT).

---

* See www.guardian.co.uk.

Please Send My Sister a Dress

Many people welcomed a fresh start in the new millennium and while cultural norms were changing dramatically, particularly in Western society, church-goers were putting away suits and dressing casual enough for a ballgame. So it seemed strange that a family packed a shoebox with a beautiful dress and matching shoes. Perhaps they knew that in other parts of the world "dressing up" was a privilege, but most never have such luxury.

In the Philippines, a Christian school was the recipient of shoebox gifts entrusted to the faculty to distribute. Using every opportunity to instill in the children God's love for them and His provision, teachers began instructing the children about giving, even out of their own poverty, and how to receive with thankful hearts. While they wanted them to anticipate the coming shoebox delivery, they explained how the boxes are packed by other children and families who pray for those who will receive them.

"Ask, and it will be given," (Matt. 7:7) deserves responsible teaching, and this school certainly seemed to be wise in doing so. The children were encouraged to begin praying for the people who had packed and sent the boxes. Then the teachers took it one step further when they said, "Pray that you will see God's provision in the items you receive, and then enjoy the generosity of Christians who have remembered you."

The day the shoeboxes arrived, an eight-year-old girl prayed before she opened her box and said, "Please send my little sister a dress." The teachers standing near were amazed at the selfless request and choked back the tears, noticing that she had been handed a box marked for a girl her age; not for a sister considerably younger.

Carefully, the little girl lifted the lid. Her eyes grew big when she pulled out a brand new dress that would perfectly fit her sister, age one. She jumped for joy and said, "I knew it, I knew it," as she looked up toward Heaven and said *"salamat"* (thank you). Did the packers mistake the age category they had chosen? There is no way to answer that question, but what can be said is that God answered the selfless prayer of a big sister who had a very big heart.

THE MISTAKE WAS JUST RIGHT

Logistics are intricate for Operation Christmas Child. The team gives careful attention to every step to prevent mistakes. But no matter how much effort goes into a distribution, boxes can sometimes be mismarked, causing a box to fall into the hands of the wrong age or gender.

Whatever the case, a little girl from Bekoso in the Ivory Coast who comes from a poor farming family, was invited to a church to receive a shoebox.

Sometime later, our team learned that the little girl had received a shoebox for an infant, containing feeding bottles, diapers, blankets and other items. She didn't complain but accepted the gift, said *"me daa si"* (thank you) and returned home.*

The very next week her mother gave birth to her little sister and when she presented the gift to her mother, it moved the mother's heart so much that she began taking the little girl to church and accepted Christ as her Savior.

It isn't hard to believe that the Lord looked down on that little girl's heart and blessed her selflessness by giving her the greater gift—salvation and a new way of life.

* OCC no longer collects boxes for infants.

In the Wake of 9/11

G reat promise was ahead for child evangelism in countries and territories we had prayed would open to us. Summer gave way to autumn, kids returned to school, and OCC season ramped up with thrilling possibilities ahead. Then terror rocked the nation—and the world. A wakeup call had come to America on 9/11.

Nations mourned with the United States and war loomed. Christians held firmly that in spite of vicious attacks on New York, Washington, D.C., and Pennsylvania, we would be faithful to proclaim that the only hope for a sin-sick world is found in Jesus Christ. Overnight, it seemed, doors for the Gospel cracked open to countries that had been closed. International churches were asking us to come and help them. We crossed the threshold into a very different world, armed with shoeboxes for kids.

Wherever our teams traveled, they were met by joyful sounds from children who began hearing, and understanding, the Christmas message. Vehicles carried thousands of shoeboxes for children who typically passed the time playing with rocks and rubbish along the Syrian border.

Afghan children playing in the dust at the Mile Forty-Six refugee camp paused to look up at the convoy of buses and trucks that arrived at the tent settlement near the Iranian border. In one location, a government official explained to the audience that some of the gifts had come from New York children—children who had also suffered at the hands of terrorists. "These gifts," he said, "are from Christians in the West. They want you to know that God has not forgotten you."

Some children were puzzled at first by the plush toy lambs because they had never seen cuddly toys. Stuffed animals had been previously outlawed by regimes. Lambs are in abundance in the Middle East, but to have one that "sings" is a special treat to little ones. When a young girl heard the musical lamb, she had probably never heard "Jesus Loves Me." Hearts of "little lambs" are in need of the nourishing love and forgiveness of the Great Shepherd, and our aim is to bring this message to them.

THE LOST BOYS OF SUDAN

South Sudan could relate to the horrors of evil. Freedom seemed a long way off for the nation and for the Lost Boys of Sudan. Their story became an international headline when the United States government sponsored thirty-six hundred of the thirty-six thousand orphans to begin new lives in America. When one of these boys stepped off the plane onto United States soil shortly before 9/11, he was wearing shoes found of all places—in a shoebox.

At the tender age of eight, this Sudanese boy began an extraordinary journey that would eventually give him a passion to help hurting children. On a fateful night in 1988, James Luom watched in terror as militants attacked his Christian village, killing the men and carrying the women off into slavery. James ran off into the bush and soon joined thirty-six thousand other boys making a mass exodus from southern Sudan.

The four-year journey of these "Lost Boys" led to Ethiopia, back to Sudan, and finally to Kenya. Thousands died from starvation, dehydration, disease, raging rivers, wild animals, and enemy soldiers. Ten thousand emaciated survivors stumbled into the Kakuma refugee camp in northern Kenya. There they would spend the remainder of their childhood surviving on just one meal a day.

One day the Lost Boys received a heartwarming surprise—shoeboxes. Inside one of those boxes was the first pair of shoes James had ever owned. "I thanked God for this gift," James recalled. "It made me feel I was loved."

James was among the boys selected to come to America in 2001, shortly before 9/11. You could say that the shoes on his feet had made a remarkable trip, for they were the white sandals he unpacked from an OCC shoebox received when he was at the Kenyan orphanage.

Now living in North Carolina, James attends college and works in ministry at a Charlotte church. When his church packed shoebox gifts a few years later, James welcomed the opportunity to send his own gift that I personally delivered for him. It went to a five-year-old Sudanese boy, a shepherd's son awaiting surgery in a Khartoum hospital. The gift from the once-orphaned boy, to another boy whose father stood at his side, represented the true meaning of grateful giving that reaps joy and blessings from God.

So as our team traveled to Afghanistan, they naturally had these kinds of stories in mind. They didn't have to look far to find many other lost boys and girls. Ten-year-old Amonaloh whose father was killed, received a shoebox gift from New York, one of thousands collected by a firefighter who took part in rescue efforts at Ground Zero on 9/11.

Hearing this young boy say *"tashakor"* (thank you) softened hearts and opened eyes to the oppression of the Afghan people. Out of the devastation and heartache that took place on that fateful day, came a glimmer of hope to share the story of Jesus with people who knew so little about another world—the kingdom of God.

Tumultuous 2001 left indelible marks on the memories of all who watched the horrors of that September morning. While we can never forget how it changed our world, Samaritan's Purse went beyond unfriendly governments in order to reach out with God's love to people who longed for peace and searched for truth.

"Do not be afraid, for behold, I bring you good tidings of great joy which will be to all people. For there is born to you . . . a Savior, who is Christ the Lord" (Luke 2:10–11).

THE BIG APPLE RESPONDS

New York, New York, was the location for a mighty big airlift of shoeboxes to Africa. It seemed natural to begin 2002 with a plan to gear up for another Operation Christmas Child season by doing something really significant. After all, the city had been hit hard by 9/11 the year before, but New Yorkers were anxious to help others in need.

The management at JFK International Airport went all out to help us stage our press conference, giving us a special ramp and allowing our invited guests to come through security with no hitches.

Our thoughts were not far from Ground Zero, a short distance away, and we were honored to be welcomed so warmly to the Big Apple by New York police and firefighters. Joining me for the event was Senator Bill Frist who addressed the crowd, international recording artist Bono who also spoke and commended the enormous effort to help kids in Africa, and the Brooklyn Tabernacle Youth Choir—they thrilled the audience with their music and enthusiasm. To the families present who had experienced great personal loss, they felt a sense of Christmas cheer knowing that our event was in remembrance of the tragedy that had taken place on 9/11.

But the incredible sight of the world's largest airplane on the ramp—the awesome Russian Antonov 225—was something really huge. It was a history-making event; this was the first time the plane had flown to the United States. It thrilled the crowd to watch as children formed a human chain to help load eighty thousand shoebox gifts aboard this giant cargo jet. Equally thrilling was to watch it liftoff—destination: Uganda.

The OCC team was already in place when the great shipment of shoeboxes arrived. Janet Museveni, the wife of Uganda's president, graciously welcomed us to her beautiful country and even helped us in our distributions, delighting the children with her warmth, conversation, and gifts. Her compassion was demonstrated in how she drew hundreds of abandoned kids around her—children who had been rescued from the streets of the capital city of Kampala.

Because of poverty and illness, many children in Uganda—especially those with HIV/AIDS—had never had the opportunity to truly celebrate Christmas. "They haven't lost being children, even when they've lived in very difficult circumstances," the First Lady said. "They're still children. I thank God for Samaritan's Purse [partners]—who make themselves willing disciples to bring happiness to these children."

NOT QUITE EMPTY

My son Roy loves to help people and he has a real heart for children. I appreciated his willingness to represent me in Central America. He and his wife, Donna, traveled to Panama for a shoebox distribution in January 2002. Once in the country, they boarded a commuter plane and flew to the little town of David (pronounced "Da-veed") where they did a series of shoebox distributions.

Before the team unloaded the boxes for their last distribution of the day, Roy led the team in prayer asking that the boxes would be guided to the right children and asking that there would be enough gifts to go around.

The children were excited as the gifts were handed out. But Roy began to feel uneasy when there appeared to be more children waiting for boxes than what was stacked up. Sure enough, they were fourteen boxes short, for ten- to fifteen-year-old boys.

Roy said, "All I could think about was watching the boys walk away empty-handed, while all the other children were jumping for joy. We had prayed this wouldn't happen!"

The team began clearing things out as the distribution came to a close, while someone wrote down the boys' names that were leaving without a gift. Roy began giving empty cardboard cartons (that the shoeboxes had been shipped in) to mothers to use for sleeping mats in their grass huts. But when Roy picked up the last carton to give away, it wasn't empty—he found exactly fourteen shoeboxes for the correct age and gender. Roy, who loves helping people, was thrilled to put those shoeboxes into the boys' hands, knowing that the Lord had answered prayer.

PARENTS IN A SHOEBOX

Surprises are always expected around Samaritan's Purse, so to hear stories from around the world about how boxes and cartons are used, and what comes out of the shoeboxes, is always fun.

Before we began documenting stories of how God was working through Operation Christmas Child, there were stories about families who packed shoeboxes and ended up adopting children who had received their boxes. God's hand was so evident in masterfully bringing these miracles about. One such story came when a little girl wrote thanking us for what she found in her shoebox—parents.

We were inspired by the story about a young couple who longed for a child. They decided to put their own desires aside and look for a way to bring joy to children out of their reach. That's when they began their journey with OCC. They took to heart our emphasis on prayer, and as they purchased items to fill a "girl box" they prayed that God would help them select just the right items.

"Lord, you know who will get this box and you know her need. We pray for this little one that you love . . . may she sense Your love through us and may You use something here to bring her some happiness and truth, wherever she may be."

They loved the program because it extended their arms beyond their walls. With great care, they filled the box and added their picture with a note that said, "You are loved. May Jesus bless you in a special way." They sealed the box and sent it on its way. But "out of sight out of mind" for them was not the case. They only hoped that the girl would understand their note and write back. They had no way of knowing that their box would find its way to an orphanage in the world's largest landlocked country.

One would think that any child living in a remote village in Central Asia would be thrilled to get a gift. But when the little orphan girl received her box, she thanked the house mother who was nearby, but left the box unopened.

"Don't you think there's something inside you'll like?" the woman asked. In her own language, the little girl replied, "Oh, thank you for the gift, but what I need is parents, that's what I really want."

The housemother said, "Well, let's just pray and ask the Lord about this." When she said "Amen," they pillaged through the box of brightly colored toys. The little girl kept saying, '*paxmet, paxmet*' (thank you), but with little enthusiasm. That is, until a picture emerged. The woman held it up in front of the child's sad face and said, "This is the family who sent you this box in Jesus' name. They cared enough to pack this box especially for you. Oh they may not know you, but this box comes with prayers just for you."

When the girl heard the word "family," she fixed her big eyes on the snapshot of the man and woman and eagerly listened as their note was read. She began to smile when the house mother asked, "Would you like to write them and say thank you?" Taking the paper and crayons from the shoebox, the little girl wrote and told the young couple how she had been praying to God for parents.

Can you just imagine what came over this husband and wife when they received such a note months later? They began corresponding with the girl. It wasn't long before the letters were not enough. Instead of slipping notes inside envelopes and mailing them, they slipped aboard a jetliner and crossed the ocean, making a visit to the orphanage to see their little pen pal. Their hearts were instantly "knit together in love," (Col. 2:2) and in time, they successfully adopted her. Through God's provision, the girl and the young couple became a family through an answered prayer, carried in a cardboard box.

If this couple had tried to orchestrate such a story, they couldn't have. This is clearly the imprint of God's love. He demonstrates His heart in ways that we often miss because we aren't praying and asking Him to show us His power. Here is a couple whose giving hearts had no ulterior motive. They hadn't set out on a mission to adopt a child half way around the world; they just simply wanted to be part of spreading God's love to others, and their new daughter was very thankful.

HOME: UNDER THE STREETS OF THE CITY

H ilario did not have a thankful heart. Our regional director for the Caribbean and Latin America told the story about this boy who had been born to a drug-addicted mother in Mexico. He never knew his father and by the time he was six, he was on his own. Some said he lived on the streets, but reality was that he lived under the streets, in the drainage pipes beneath the city. By Hilario's ninth birthday, he was stealing from some, dealing to others, and beating anyone who got in his way. The drug community was his world and it didn't take him long to find a new home in a juvenile detention center, making an orphanage look like home sweet home. Through his teen years he was in and out of prison and became a hardened and angry young man.

Hilario derived satisfaction in climbing the ladder, all the way to the highest security prison in Mexico. He became involved in a movement inside the prison of "worshiping death." With just a look, Hilario got whatever he demanded from his fellow prisoners; even the guards feared him.

I have visited prisons around the world. They are dungeons of darkness. Perhaps this is why Jesus stood in the synagogue and read from the book of Isaiah, "The Spirit of the Lord is on me . . . He has sent me to proclaim freedom for the prisoners" (Luke 4:18 NIV). No matter where I go in the world, no matter how dangerous or remote, God has His people.

Prison ministry is something that most people never experience. Yet it is an area of ministry the Lord commends. What a testimony, then, to hear about Pastor Reynaldo, one of our partners with a heart for prisoners.

He began holding meetings inside the prison that was home to Hilario. With Bible and guitar in hand, Reynaldo and his brother David went every Wednesday to share the Gospel. While the message tenderized many inmates, the Gospel truth stirred Hilario up with anger, leading him to devise a plot to kill the pastor.

"I went to my cell," he wrote later, "and pulled out my hidden knife. I proceeded to the center courtyard and made my intentions clear to the preacher—he was going to die that day! Pastor stood there without flinching. Then he said something that changed my life: 'Hilario, why would you hurt me? I came here because of the love that God has given me for you—and God loves you too.'"

This prisoner turned and ran to his cell, tears drenching his face and hands. The words "I love you" broke through his imprisoned heart. That very day, the Gospel message of Christ's love freed Hilario. He repented of his sin. The evidence of a changed life was so clear, as in the story of Zacchaeus, when Hilario repaid all those he had robbed within the prison walls. His twenty-one-year sentence took on a new purpose and as Reynaldo taught him from the Scriptures, Hilario Morales began sharing his newfound faith with all those around him.

Sometime later, this transformed prisoner was released and his sentence reduced, for no apparent reason. Hilario walked out a free man. In times past when he had been released from other prisons, he walked out alone. But on this day, two brothers were waiting. Hilario, this one-time orphan boy, was invited to a new home by his brothers-in-Christ, Pastor Reynaldo and David. They took him to their house and for the first time in his life, Hilario experienced the nurturing of home and family, a place where God his Father was reverenced and served. He never ceases saying to his new family and Father in Heaven, *"gracias"* (thank you).

You may be asking what this has to do with Operation Christmas Child. Hilario married Reynaldo's cousin and together they have been serving through OCC in Guadalajara. They have planted a church, started an orphanage for children of prisoners and street kids, and have coordinated and managed shoebox distributions throughout the region, preaching the Gospel and teaching thousands of children, using our discipleship materials. This is the transforming power that is offered by the Christmas Child to a convicted child, who became a converted child of the King.

WHY GOSPEL PEOPLE LOVE TO GIVE

We love our OCC volunteers—and there are tens of thousands! These are dedicated people around the world who have been recruited, selected, and trained. But they would tell you that they have also been called by God to serve Him through Operation Christmas Child. When they come on board, their spiritual gifts are matched with their given responsibilities and then they are equipped. They give their time and abilities in a variety of ways, but what they all have in common is their love for kids, their desire to spread the Gospel, and to be prayer warriors in winning souls to Jesus Christ. Most of all, they are givers.

Richard Bewes wrote an article for us on the subject of giving our time and resources. This retired rector of All Souls Church in London, England, member of our board of directors, and friend wrote:

> The reason why people of the Gospel are givers is that giving has everything to do with a heart that has been touched by God. Over two centuries ago, the evangelist John Wesley wrote to his sister, Patty Hall: "Money never stays with me; it would burn me if it did. I throw it out of my hands as soon as possible, lest it should find a way into my heart." It's the heart that is vital. God wants hearts, not coins! We preachers sometimes declare that the pocket is the last part of the Christian to be converted. The Bible disagrees. The pocket is converted along with everything else—speech, relationships, priorities.

Grateful people make generous givers. God—the greatest giver of all—makes it His business to multiply the effectiveness of His people's giving, to make it stretch in ways that they would not have thought possible. "I will not sacrifice to the Lord my God [that which] cost me nothing" (2 Sam. 24:24 NIV).

God has touched the hearts of givers to help us expand our child evangelism outreach. When we experienced remarkable growth and had outgrown our facilities in Boone, we were able to build a facility at Samaritan's Purse headquarters to house the OCC team, provide adequate warehouse space, and establish a new processing center.

Shortly before National Collection Week 2004, our OCC team moved into a new hub that has become a frequent destination for enthusiastic supporters. God's truth is that, "It is more blessed to give than to receive" (Acts 20:35).

THAT MUSTY OL' SHOEBOX

G iving is the heart of the Christmas story, because giving is an attribute of Jesus, and Christians are called to follow His ways.

We saw this demonstrated through an anonymous package. During a meeting with my staff in January 2004, my secretary slipped out of the room to investigate some commotion in the outer office. A minute or two later she walked back in with Humphrey Hayes, head of security. I knew something was up.

Humphrey is a mountain of a man and one of few words. His countenance is steadfast, so I couldn't tell if he had good news or bad. He put a shoebox in my hand with crinkled brown paper hanging by shreds. "You'll want to see this," that's all he said.

The box had obviously been on quite a journey. I remembered the brown paper-wrapped box that Carol Rhoads had found in Bosnia that held a bountiful gift. So my curiosity was piqued to think that this brown paper box was escorted to my office by Humphrey.

When I learned what was inside the box, I understood the ruckus moments before. The box had been sent to me at our Charlotte processing center with the same address in the left corner. The post office had delivered it just after Christmas while the staff was closing the temporary facility. John Pryor, our PC (processing center) manager in Charlotte put the box, along with another, in his car to bring to Boone.

Days later when John cleaned out his backseat, he saw the boxes and delivered them to Donald Critcher, our PC manager in Boone. He and some others had been talking through the layout of the new warehouse and processing center being built for OCC. Casually, Donald sketched out his idea on the brown paper box. Afterward, he sliced through the brown wrapping, perhaps the remnant of a grocery bag, and lifted the lid. It reeked with antiquity; crinkled tissue paper concealed the contents. When he pulled the paper away, this tranquil man became pale.

Packed tightly from end to end were stacks of one-hundred dollar bills, bundled and bound with rubber bill straps; many were broken and stuck to the paper. Between the rotten bands and the musty odor, we concluded that the money had been stored a very long time, perhaps twenty years, inside a mattress, in a safe, or hidden in shoes as old and musty as the shoebox.

Donald and John walked the box over to Bob Cook and Keith Perry who managed our World Medical Mission warehouse. "You guys aren't gonna believe what's in here," Donald said, still gaping. Bob took one look and said, "You better call Humphrey."

When Humphrey walked in, these strong and robust guys were standing back from the box as though a rattle snake was inside. Humphrey assessed the situation and said, "Come on John, let's take it to the president's office."

So, here we were with the box—a shoebox. I removed the lid and was stunned to see the bundles of cash, particularly since we always make a concerted effort to encourage donors to send checks, not cash. But this particular donor's clear intention was to remain anonymous.

I slid the box over to Phyllis Payne, vice president of Finance. She gazed at the contents and flipped through a band or two, then put the lid in place. "Many thousands of dollars," Phyllis said in her gentle matter-of-fact way. Humphrey delivered the box to the appropriate people where it was counted and then taken to the bank for deposit. God had protected that box which could have represented someone's life's savings—almost $75,000.

No letter could be written. No call could be made. No receipt could be mailed. It troubled me that there was no one to thank. Then I remembered how we had started our meeting that morning—asking the Lord to lead us into another year of ministry; multiplying our resources to reach a greater value in souls saved. He answered that prayer.

"For God . . . will provide and increase your resources and then produce a great harvest of generosity in you . . . and when we take your gifts to those who need them, they will thank God" (2 Cor. 9:10–11 NLT).

Super-glued to Connie

Most kids in Western societies have what they "need," maybe not all that they want. Ask most kids today what they would like to find under the Christmas tree and the answers will likely be an iPod, a cell phone, or an array of gift cards that will allow them to do their own shopping. But for Livia Satterfield who grew up in a Romania orphanage, it didn't matter that there was no Christmas tree. She had many needs, but all she wanted was something very simple and practical, but no one was listening.

Livia had been abandoned by her parents (as many children in Romania experienced). With no one to confide in, her loneliness turned to jealousy and anger. She didn't know how to accept love or give it.

"I grew up taking baths in dirty water and wearing the same clothes for weeks at a time," Livia said as she shared her testimony of what the Lord had done for her. "If visitors came with gifts for the children, they would be confiscated later. I learned not to hope for anything and I knew not to expect anything good," she said.

Then she heard that shoebox gifts were coming for the orphans. Could she dare hope again and dream that she might get something she had longed for—hairclips? She wasn't aware at the time that "Someone" had looked into her heart and understood her desire, but also knew her deepest need.

Livia told us later,

The big day arrived . . . a very big day that warmed my heart. It was even warm outside and things just seemed better, yet I didn't know why. Then I saw a bus pull up with a team of people from the United States. A lady from Newnan, Georgia, stepped off the bus and I instantly latched on to her. She was among a team of people who helped distribute shoebox gifts from Operation Christmas Child. I knew this would be my only chance to get someone to hold my hand, to talk to me. And Connie did. I didn't know how long she would be there, so I wanted my moment in time.

I monopolized her attention. I was "super-glued" to Connie and would not share her with anyone else. I was desperate for love; I was obsessed with it and I wanted Connie to be all mine. I told the other kids who came around to go away.

When time came to distribute the shoeboxes, Connie and others first wanted to share with us a message. We were eager to hear anything they had to say, just to have someone talking to us and caring for us was a gift. We had heard of Jesus but we didn't know much about Him. We had been taught to use the sign of the cross over our bodies and kiss the pictures of Jesus and Mary, but we didn't know the meaning. Why was He on the cross? We didn't understand. Hearing the message from the missionaries began to open my understanding.

Then, before we opened the boxes, we were told that the boxes had been "packed with prayer and love, and given in Jesus' name." I was sitting there at twelve years old trying to figure out how a person who packed this box could know me and love me? They had never seen me face-to-face. They didn't know my name. And how do you pack a box with prayer? We were shown a bracelet with colored beads: black that stands for sin, red for the blood that Jesus shed on the cross to forgive our sins, white signifying we could be made clean if we were washed free of our sins by His blood. I began to understand that He loves me and wants to forgive me for the awful things I had done—the stealing, the hatefulness, and the jealousy—all that stems from sin against God; He loved me in spite of my sinfulness and though I could not see

Him face-to-face, He knew my name and He knew I needed love; and He wanted me to love Him!

This brand new story was going around in my head as Connie and the others began counting: "One, two, three . . ." That was our cue to open our boxes.

It occurred to me later that the anticipation and exhilaration of that moment was like shaking a Coke bottle and then opening it as the liquid bursts and covers you. The thrill was that explosive.

The first thing I saw when I lifted the lid of my shoebox was a big pack of hair clips in a variety of sizes and colors. I couldn't believe it! I had very short hair, but immediately I put every one of the clips in my hair. Connie watched in disbelief. She tried to persuade me to use just two, one on each side of my head. But no! My whole head was covered. There were many things in the box, but other items that stood out were the hygiene items that included a toothbrush and toothpaste. When we did get to brush our teeth, we had to share a toothbrush, so to have my very own was something hard to comprehend. I began to realize that God was pouring so many things into my life.

When I thought I had reached the bottom of the box, I discovered a necklace. It was a heart broken in half. I later learned it was a "best friend's necklace," one part pink, the other yellow. I wanted Connie to know how much it meant to me that she would show me love. I gave her one half of the necklace and told her, "Maybe one day we can put the hearts together." To my surprise, I learned later that God had put it on her heart to adopt me. Two years later, Connie came back for me and our hearts were united in a way I could have never imagined.

I've been living in the United States since then but have never forgotten being rescued from despair and finding salvation in the Lord Jesus Christ. I returned to Romania with OCC to distribute shoeboxes to other orphans and tell them, in their language, what Jesus had done for me, and what He will do for them. I also met my biological mother whom I had not seen since the age of three. I told her about Christ who lives in me and gave her a New Testament. She said she could see the difference in Christians and non-Christians. My prayer is that she will be saved and come to know the difference that Christ makes in broken hearts. I thank God for the opportunity OCC gives me to share my story with so many, praying that it will point others to Him.

This is the evidence of "packing a box with prayer." God blesses these stories with truth—that Jesus came to heal sinful and broken hearts. Livia learned that packing a box with prayer meant that God had empowered the intent of the giver to point the receiver to the Savior.

"Blessed be God, who has not turned away my prayer" (Ps. 66:20).

SCHOOL NUMBER ONE

Terror struck Beslan, Russia, when a group of armed militants seized and occupied School Number One (SNO) taking children and faculty hostage on the first day of school in 2004. After three days of horror, the conflict ended tragically when over three hundred and forty-four hostages were killed, among them one hundred and seventy children. Others went missing and many were severely injured. This small town nestled in the shadows of the Caucasus Mountains will never be the same.

Just a few weeks before the siege and massacre, Operation Christmas Child did a program at the school, distributing shoebox gifts along with *The Greatest Gift of All* booklet, followed by the invitation for students to enroll in the OCC discipleship program.

Ten-year-old Arthur was one of those students who attended the program and enrolled in the course. When Arthur's mother took him to school the day of the attack, she had no idea that he would never come home again; Arthur was among the children who lost their lives. When his papers were found later, his mother said that he had indicated that he had put his faith and trust in Christ. In the days that followed, there were accounts of Arthur praying and comforting children and adults during the siege and hostage crisis.

We returned to Beslan later that year with more shoeboxes as a demonstration of our deep concern for the children who had survived. The repercussions of the Columbine school shooting in the United States came to mind and we asked Crystal Woodman-Miller, a survivor of that school shooting, to join the OCC team. She was used to bring comfort to the students and said, "These shoeboxes represent light in a dark place. My hope is that through the gifts, letters, and pictures each will feel the love of Jesus, and sense the love and support from those praying for them."

When the team arrived at the school, they were astounded to see the big Samaritan's Purse cartons sitting in the basement of the school left over from the distribution that had been done earlier that year. It seemed a bold symbol of remembrance that God's Word had visited that place.

THE SILVER CHALLENGE

Children are impressionable and easily influenced. I can remember as a boy being fascinated by men who always had pockets full of change. As they stood talking, they would stick their hands in their pockets and jingle the change. Back then (I'm showing my age) almost everything was bought with cash, so it was normal at the end of the day to have a pocket full of change.

Today, very few carry cash; it's been replaced by plastic. Teachers who love OCC have been very creative in showing kids how they can help other kids who live very different lives. One school who values its students taught them how to value small change: nickels, dimes and quarters. They instigated "The Silver Challenge," as a way to support shoeboxes for kids.

When children are taught the joy of giving, most catch on quickly. Creative giving can be fun, especially when they do it willingly. To force children to give, or to use peer pressure, can defeat the lesson of becoming a cheerful giver.

The faculty put a good deal of thought into inspiring the kids to give, inviting them to donate their silver change left over after lunch. The cafeteria became the collection center, with shoeboxes placed at the end of the checkout counter. Another shoebox was filled with silver coins, allowing the students to redeem their copper pennies for silver.

Teachers taught about different parts of the world, countries destined for shoebox distributions. The more kids learned about children in other places, the more sales of ice cream and sodas dropped and silver change increased. Students were giving up extras when they learned that kids in other countries seldom—or never—had such treats. In fact, they were shocked to learn that many kids have never known the satisfaction of drinking clean water.

How did the challenge end up?

"Dear OCC," the letter said, "Enclosed is our check for $2,500 to be used to cover the cost of sending some shoeboxes around the world."

The recipients of these boxes can truly say, "Silver and gold have we none" (Acts 3:6), but they were blessed by God who provided, through others, the joy of receiving; and the young givers made a difference in the lives of many with their nickels and dimes.

CHRISTMAS BOXES
FOR EASTER

People enjoy the power of money; however many do not realize the eternal impact it can have when it is given to spread the Gospel. The Bible says that the Gospel is the power unto salvation (Rom. 1:16). This is the power of the shoebox.

By 2005, reports were coming in that *The Greatest Gift of All* was being read and studied not only by children but by parents, teachers, and others throughout communities visited by Operation Christmas Child. We were providing local churches with a Bible study course that pastors could use to teach others about God's Word and what it means to become a faithful follower of Jesus Christ. We could have never guessed that doors would open to places like Indonesia for this kind of ministry.

When the 2004 tsunami wiped out huge populations in nations along the Indian Ocean the day after Christmas, the world watched with stunning awe at the destruction and death toll. Reported as the third largest earthquake ever recorded, it triggered other earthquakes as far away as Alaska. The world responded with aid. Samaritan's Purse was on the ground within hours waiting to gain access to the region with medicine, food, and shelter. OCC began making plans to help the children.

The first special Easter collection of shoeboxes provided gifts for two hundred and seventy thousand children—survivors of the nightmare that raged in memory. Prayers were answered as we heard from children around the world; their enthusiasm for the Gospel was contagious. Hope replaced fear. One child wrote and said, "I told my mother what I learned about Jesus, and now I don't have to go alone to church, my mother comes too because she has also received Him."

OCC wasn't about building a team or erecting a building, OCC was about building upon the Word of God. While shoebox numbers mounted, testimonies were being built upon God's truth and how He was using the shoebox gifts to demonstrate His love to a shattered world.

SHOEBOX DIGGIN' SPADE

The headquarters of Samaritan's Purse is cradled in the western mountains of North Carolina. No one can find us just off an interstate exit, so it is surprising how many visitors make the trek up the Blue Ridge Parkway to see us. There are those who come to see the World Medical Mission operation, others enjoy learning more about the projects we are involved in worldwide, and many come to see Operation Christmas Child in action.

Virginia "Ginny" Cook is one of those people. She made an impromptu visit to OCC on her way back from Florida to Ohio. Instead of the quick tour she expected, she stayed two days to help with our Easter collection for the victims of the tsunami. When she heard stories of how shoeboxes were impacting volunteers on this side of the shoebox, and how children were impacted on the other side of the box, God touched her heart to do more than just take a peek at the operation. She inquired about helping in a more significant way and was put in touch with Bonnie Freeman, our regional director for the Great Lakes.

Ginny is now our regional volunteer coordinator, covering ten counties that border the Ohio River. Ten percent of the US population lives in the Ohio River Basin. Ginny is proud of her Southeast Ohio heritage and loves to talk about the beautiful river "ringed round with glorious hills that look down upon valleys and fields, where the corn grows high and dairy cows graze in lush meadows." Ginny has said, "Folks in this area have been diggin' in the dirt for generations and we don't seem to stray too far from where we are planted."

This lady may be retired, but she isn't tired. In fact, she's hard to keep up with. The prayer coordinator in the area called her one day and gave her the Scripture verse, "I say unto you, he that believes in Me, the works that I do he will do also" (John 14:12).

Ginny's a worker and a planter of Gospel seed. She works with local churches throughout the fertile landscape and calls her shoe-box diggin' spade a tool in God's hand to stir people of faith—to come and help plant the seed of the Gospel in hearts from Ohio to oceans beyond that great river.

To Timbuktu and Back

The Niger River is the pride of Mali, West Africa; in fact, it is Mali's life-blood. Its citizens say, "We could not live without the river." Just as those who live along the Ohio are thrilled to pack shoeboxes for places faraway, we were equally thrilled to send shoeboxes to Mali's most mysterious city—Timbuktu. Many think it is a fictional place, but it is more than just legend.

The first European to reach Timbuktu was a Scottish explorer who didn't live to tell about it. Alexander Gordon Laing was killed in 1826 by tribal zealots who feared that the mere footprints of a Christian would desecrate their holy city.

Almost thirty years later, a German named Heinrich Barth became famous by trekking across the Sahara Desert to Timbuktu and returning safely, thus the adage, "to Timbuktu and back." He described his odyssey as a series of miracles. "The first miracle," Barth said, "is to believe Timbuktu exists." Even in the twenty-first century, the name Timbuktu conjures up the idea of edge-of-the-world isolation.

Timbuktu, though, really exists and once was the capital of a vast empire. Today, shrouded in the encroaching sands of the Sahara, it survives as an impoverished little city with a poetic name.

Over three thousand children in Timbuktu had a unique opportunity to discover the true meaning of Christmas—the birth of Jesus Christ—thanks to an unprecedented journey by Operation Christmas Child.

A distribution was done at a school where ordinary evangelism would have been virtually impossible. However, the headmaster was so delighted by the gifts that he also gave permission for each child to take home a Gospel storybook in French, the national language of Mali. A pastor there thanked us and said, "OCC is helping us bring the Gospel to places where we otherwise could not enter."

There are only about two hundred Christians in the population of about forty thousand, so most of the children and families have no concept of Christmas, much less the Person of Jesus Christ, according to a local pastor who converted to Christianity in the late sixties. He discovered the truth of the Bible after a missionary offered him a small gift—a clicking ballpoint pen—as an incentive to memorize Scripture.

Basic school supplies like those in the shoeboxes are highly prized in Timbuktu, especially by children from destitute nomadic families who have pitched their tents around the town in settlements known as the "Belt of Misery."

That's a far cry from the Timbuktu of antiquity, which earned its fame through prosperity and education. Camel caravans came hundreds of miles from across Africa to trade gold, salt, and slaves. The Sankore Mosque became one of the world's first universities, with a library of over thirty thousand manuscripts. Legends spread that Timbuktu was so rich that even the desert sands were made of gold.

Inevitably, the city was attacked and plundered. By the time the first Europeans arrived, the only vestige of Timbuktu's glory days were three mosques, including one that dates back to the tenth century.

Timbuktu, though, is not easy to reach. For OCC, the journey involved four thousand miles by ship across the Atlantic from Charleston to Dakar, and then one thousand miles by truck across Senegal and Mali. Much of the road is unpaved and prone to bandits, so the just-in-time arrival of the gifts was an answer to prayer.

Among these boxes was one packed by five-year-old Harry, for a boy his age. "We hoped it would go somewhere far away and to someone that needed to hear the message of God," his mother said. Had they tried to orchestrate sending it to Timbuktu, it would have been impossible. But that's just where God sent it.

Harry's box was given to a boy named Ahmed who lived with his grandmother. Ahmed marveled at the Etch-a-Sketch and delighted in the hard candy, but nothing touched his heart quite like the letter and snapshot from Harry. And I wouldn't doubt for a minute that when Ahmed gazed at little Harry's picture, he saw his great big heart with lots of love from a great big God.

As the apostle Paul wrote, "You show that you are a letter from Christ, the result of our ministry, written not with ink but with the Spirit of the living God, not on tablets of stone but on tablets of human hearts" (2 Cor. 3:3 NIV).

The pastor stated how critical it is to reach this generation of children with the Gospel. The Christians of Timbuktu are praying for the dawn of a glory that outshines anything their city has ever known and bring Timbuktu back to the God of all creation. From the simple gift of a pen from a missionary given to this man searching for truth, the Gospel has gained entrance into one of the most secluded regions on earth. This small congregation of believers needs the prayers of the church around the world as they face incomprehensible challenges, but are so faithful to God's calling to be a witness for Him.

"The wilderness and the wasteland shall be glad for them, and the desert shall rejoice and blossom as the rose . . . they shall see the glory of the LORD, the excellency of our God" (Isa. 35:1–2).

No Reservation for the Apache Chief

Legends are full of intrigue, but in the case of Reynard Faber, honorary chieftain of the Jicarilla Apache Nation in Dulce, New Mexico, and great grandson of the Apache chief Geronimo, his life was one of inability. But when he heard the Gospel, he had no reservations in trading his religion as tribal medicine man for faith in Christ.

Reynard serves with the Native American Distribution Division of Operation Christmas Child and has been instrumental in opening the gateways to American Indians. He represents thousands of members of his tribe on a one million acre reservation in Northern New Mexico, where only 5 percent of his people are professed Christians.

Samaritan's Purse has reached out to thousands of children who perhaps would never hear the name Jesus were it not for the shoeboxes. Wings of Eagles Ministries partnered with OCC for a 2006 distribution of shoeboxes at Little Wound School. Located on the Pine Ridge Indian Reservation, one hundred and twenty miles from Rapid City, South Dakota, this visit brought great hope to the people.

In consultation with Chief Reynard, we select a different reservation each year as a way to bring the Good News of the Gospel to children who suffer abuse and hunger within the borders of the United States.

A young boy wrote sometime after receiving his shoebox,

> I never heard about Jesus until you gave me this gift. When I read *The Greatest Story of All* then I understood why gifts are given at Christmas—because God sent His Son as a gift to the world. I let my parents read the booklet and

they became angry. I couldn't understand why they were unhappy when my life changed for the better because of what I learned from the shoebox distribution. When they finally listened, I told them that the booklet promised that the Holy Spirit would guide me and teach me how to live the right way. They read the book again and discovered that the "great spirit in the sky" has a name, the Holy Spirit of God. They have come to believe, also, that ritual cannot change a life, but the richness of Christ changes our spirits to reflect Him. My spirit knows I am Indian, but thank God His Spirit assures me that I am His.

THE BOOK IS PASSED ON AND ON

A few dozen shoeboxes will fill the trunk of a car. About seven thousand can be loaded in a tractor-trailer. But who can comprehend what millions look like? By 2006, the 7.6 million shoeboxes collected, if laid end to end, would stretch well over 1,400 miles. While we can count the number of boxes collected, we will never know the number of souls reached for Christ. We can count how many pieces of Gospel literature accompanies the shoeboxes, but these materials take flight, falling into hands that never even see a shoebox or know anything about it.

In a village during an OCC distribution, a very excited man approached Jim Harrelson wanting to show him something. He ran into his home and came out with a copy of *The Greatest Gift of All* booklet. We could tell by the printing that it had been distributed with shoebox gifts four years earlier at an event in Cape Haitian, a town many miles away. Yet this well-worn booklet had survived and been shared, read and passed on to others miles from its origin. It happens all the time.

A volunteer, thrilled to be part of a distribution team to Thailand, was at the airport in Bangkok on her way to a distribution. The ticket agent noticed the OCC logo on her jacket and became animated. "I'm from Burkina Faso," he said pulling something out of his pocket. It was a dog-eared copy of the same booklet. Waving it in front of her he said, "I never knew why Jesus had hung on the cross until I read this story."

It seems that OCC speaks to everyone who is paying attention, and the literature designed for children proves that Christ's message to the world is simple enough for a child, clear to those who have faith to believe, and strong enough to prepare hearts to serve Christ.

A Family Affair

Caryn Jackson may have been our youngest volunteer because she has been involved with OCC since she was just a year old, and still serves with us today.

"I really can't remember living without shoeboxes—it's been a way of life. Mom says I cut my teeth on them," Caryn said. "I was thankful to have the privilege of serving as a child, as an adolescent, and then as a teenager as part of the OCC media relations team at the age of fifteen, then traveling to Mongolia at sixteen. The potential for service with OCC is endless, and the most satisfying of all is to know that through being available to the Lord, I have learned how to share my faith in Christ with those who do not know Him. My life has been shaped by the joy of serving in this unique and exciting way."

Caryn's mother, Carla, was actually the one who was first called to the work of OCC. She was recovering from pneumonia and confined to bed. Her sister brought her a copy of *Living Beyond the Limits,* a book I had written that year that included chapters about OCC. "While I had heard of Samaritan's Purse," Carla said, "I felt like a secret had been kept from me. When my husband Jeff came home that evening I told him about some of the stories in the book and we both swept away tears. At that moment, God placed His calling on our hearts to serve in some capacity with OCC."

Carla and Jeff took the first steps and began packing shoeboxes and talking to others at their church about doing the same. With each new step of the program they jumped in all the way, traveling from Dallas, Texas, to Charlotte to help the first year we were in our Charlotte processing center.

Joey White, our PC manager in Charlotte was so grateful for this family's commitment and asked if they would consider serving on our domestic mission staff. Because the Jacksons home schooled their four children, they had the flexibility to spend several weeks each fall in Charlotte. Within two years, they were serving as relay center coordinators in Athens, Texas. By 2007, Carla was the area coordinator for East Central Texas. Keep in mind, this entire family was serving in some volunteer capacity. This is the core of OCC— God's volunteer army.

Then Carla joined a distribution team to Ecuador. "I remember ministering to children and their families who lived at the city dump and was moved with compassion as they listened intently to the Gospel account of why Jesus came and died to save lost souls."

"The most powerful memory, though, came as I was handing a shoebox to a child. My mind was suddenly flooded with the faces and voices of volunteers saying how they wished they could personally deliver their boxes—to see the look on their faces, to look into their eyes, to hug them and tell them how much Jesus loves them."

"Struggling with that vision helped me through that distribution with a deep sense of responsibility. I was representing countless people who had handled these boxes and prayed over these boxes from the packers and donors, to every pair of hands that loaded and unloaded them. I was reminded that I was an ambassador for this great army of praying people who cared for lost souls."

"If Jeff and I could have orchestrated a program that our entire family could do together, we could not have come up with anything more effective and satisfying as Operation Christmas Child."

HRH: HONORING REAL HEROES

B ritish hierarchy is good at expressing public thanks to volunteers. And OCC has many of them across the United Kingdom.

When our team in England heard that Prime Minister David Cameron had taken notice of the charitable work of volunteers through Operation Christmas Child, they extended an invitation for him to visit our warehouse in Witney, Oxfordshire. He toured the facility and delivered a gift-filled shoebox that was later carried to Belarus and given to nine-year-old Alisa, suffering with cerebral palsy.

The Prime Minister took time to meet the volunteers and encouraged them with these words, "For me one of the best things about this time of year is the way people make an extra effort to help others. It is truly heartening to meet the people here who have donated their time and money to give Christmas shoeboxes to disadvantaged children across the world through Operation Christmas Child."

Her Royal Highness Princess Anne also paid tribute to OCC volunteers when she visited our warehouse in Weston-super-Mare. The Princess Royal had commended the voluntary efforts of a family who had generously donated units at both their home and office storage company to help make OCC a big hit in the local area. She observed the shoeboxes being prepared for delivery to Belarus and expressed thanks to all those serving, to make Christmas memorable for the children.

For Operation Christmas Child, HRH also means Honoring Real Heroes—and these are our volunteers around the world who give themselves wholeheartedly to this work. Whether ladies knitting scarves and hats for the shoeboxes; whether men driving forklifts and hauling cartons; whether children packing and praying—they are touching little hearts for God. Their service in the name of Jesus touches the heart of God.

Wheelchairs Don't Climb Stairs

Every Sunday in Poland, Zanna would sit by the window in her parents' apartment and listen to music coming from the evangelical church next door. She longed to meet the people who sing so beautifully about God.

All she could do was wish, though. Many people mistakenly considered the church a cult, and her family thought visiting there might be a sin. Besides that, Zanna was partially paralyzed, and it was difficult to get her wheelchair down three flights of stairs.

One day, however, a church member saw Zanna sitting at the window. She looked lonely. The woman told the congregation about this young girl and the church began to pray. They were compelled to visit the girl who lived three flights up. When the church callers met Zanna and discovered her disability, they knew their prompting was from the Lord. Operation Christmas Child was preparing to hold a shoebox distribution at their church—a special service for handicapped children—and Zanna and her family were invited. The friendly visit overcame her parents' fears, and they accepted.

On the day of the distribution, the family received a warm greeting at the church and felt there was something special about these Christians; they were just as joyful as their music.

Zanna was overwhelmed by the love of the people in the church. When the pastor shared the Gospel, she accepted Jesus as her Savior. She was excited to receive her shoebox gift, but nothing could compare with the real gift she received that day—God's gift of eternal life and a reason for her heart to go on singing.

Bikers with Boxes

My ears are always listening for a rumble. I love motorcycles and I love their roar.

So when I heard about bikers collecting shoeboxes for Operation Christmas Child, I just had to invite them to the Billy Graham Library in Charlotte. And they came. Motorcycle clubs across the country collect shoebox gifts and ride to various locations to deliver them. You may ask how you can transport shoeboxes on motorcycles.

These bikes roared through the gates with trailers hooked to the backs of their bikes. Following close behind was a truck carrying the cartons that were too big for motorcycles.

On another occasion more than eight hundred and fifty riders rumbled into the parking lot, and what emerged from that sea of chrome and leather was nearly fifteen hundred boxes.

One Harley Davidson rider, Phillip Morris, said, "I cried from my church to here, and that's about fifty miles of tears." He had lived in rebellion for years and then the Lord got hold of his heart and changed it. He and his wife continued riding motorcycles, but instead of parking their bikes at the bars and nightclubs, they park them at church or use them to rally other bikers to deliver shoeboxes through a Christian bikers club, the Carolina Faith Riders.

Sorina Riddle met some of these bikers and melted their hearts. Sorina was the recipient of a shoebox gift when she was a young girl in Romania. Now a young adult and living in the United States, she attended a biker's rally and told them what it was like to live in Romania at Christmas in the frigid conditions.

My brother and I were invited to a church to receive gifts, so we trekked in the snow to the event, not knowing what to expect. I hoped with child-like faith that I could get something to keep me warm in the wintertime, but our family was poor. We heard about Jesus being a free gift to all who would receive Him by faith. At the end of the service, we were given shoebox gifts from OCC. When I opened my box, all that I had prayed for—and more—was there for the taking: a hat, a scarf, and gloves.

In time, Sorina accepted Christ as her Savior and was baptized. She told the bikers, "Know that your job is to pack the box and put a prayer with it, and to trust that God will direct it to meet the particular needs of a child, so that His great name will be known."

When I met Sorina, I was reminded once again of the power of a simple gift to make an eternal impact. Sorina still treasures the wool scarf, hat, and mittens she received over fifteen years ago.

Because someone cared enough to send a shoebox, Sorina had the opportunity to receive God's gift of salvation through faith in Jesus Christ. Today, she is a joyful Christian and is packing shoeboxes to send to other children.

We have seen the evidence of what the Bible says, "That Your way [Lord] may be known on earth, Your salvation among all nations" (Ps. 67:2).

PEOPLE CALL US "SHOEBOX CITY"

From a biker's club of eight hundred and fifty, to a community of less than fifteen hundred people, collecting almost twenty-one thousand shoebox gifts in 2008 was an impressive achievement.

"People call us 'Shoebox City,'" said seventy-seven-year-old Nettie Hyde, one of the primary organizers of the project in Rosebud, Texas. "The spirit of Operation Christmas Child is contagious."

Nearly everyone in town takes part in the project, from school-children to shopkeepers to nursing home residents.

The owner of a nursery donates flowers and shrubs for a community plant sale that raises money for Operation Christmas Child.

A middle-aged man who receives kidney dialysis three times a week hands out brochures at the hospital.

The mayor considers it his civic duty every November to help load cartons of shoeboxes onto trucks headed for the collection center in Waco. It is a community affair.

While thousands of people travel to "Christmas City, USA" to shop and mail their Christmas cards because of its name—Bethlehem, Pennsylvania; Christmas for the people of Rosebud, Texas, is not a destination, it's home.

Rosebud doesn't have a shopping mall or a professional sports team, but the residents there have something very special bringing them together—a huge heart for Christmas—and Operation Christmas Child.

The Greatest Journey Begins

One of the great journeys for OCC has been to explore how we can best reach kids "after the box." We don't want to just give a shoebox of toys. We want the gifts to be followed by a practical and biblical study of God's Word. He has set before us an unprecedented door of opportunity (Rev. 3:8) that no man can shut. This is the sole purpose of Operation Christmas Child—to reach out to children in Jesus' name and to communicate God's love for them.

This is what led us to begin strengthening the literature that accompanies or follows the shoebox distributions. We heard the needs from the local pastors for more follow-up materials to the boxes and evangelistic literature. We partnered with The Mailbox Club beginning in 2000 to provide the ten lesson Bible study called "Explorers One." This was our first discipleship program that followed the distribution of shoeboxes. The results were astounding with over ten million children graduating in sixty countries.

In 2007 Samaritan's Purse began developing a new discipleship program based on three distinct focuses—evangelism, discipleship, and personal evangelism. I wanted a Bible study program for children that would take them deeper into God's Word.

An international development team worked diligently for eighteen months to create appropriate materials for children and local churches in developing countries. They had traveled around the world and had gathered information from pastors and church workers who understood the depth of spiritual needs of the children.

The result was the launching of *The Greatest Journey*. This curriculum has been put into the hands of millions of children through the generosity of our donors. Its truth has changed millions of hearts.

This Bible course is packaged in one booklet with three sections containing twelve lessons. The colorful illustrations bring the Gospel to life with Scripture readings and interactive exercises. Our buddy Sam, the flying shoebox, takes children on this exciting journey as they learn about God's plan of salvation through Jesus Christ, how to follow Him faithfully and how to purposefully pray for and share their faith initially with their family and friends. They are introduced to heroes of the Bible, and discover ways to put their own faith into action.

David Thompson, director of OCC International, who has been with us since 2005, has done an excellent job in working with our international partners on *The Greatest Journey* discipleship course in the area of recruiting, selecting, and training teachers. Our OCC International team has said, "It is our hope and prayer that this emphasis will help children to recognize their key role in the Great Commission."

Four English-speaking countries in 2009 implemented the new course in pilot test groups with up to thirty groups of children per country, completing the course in order to receive helpful feedback before distributing the materials worldwide. In 2010 the course was translated into Spanish and distributed throughout Latin America, followed by a gradual phase-in of the discipleship materials in other receiving countries. In 2013, more than forty thousand volunteer teachers taught over one million boys and girls in eighty-five countries and seventy-two languages, utilizing *The Greatest Journey*! Our goal by 2017 is for five million OCC children to be participating in *The Greatest Journey.*

Those who finish the course receive personalized certificates and Bibles or New Testaments in their own language. For many, they have never owned a book of any kind. To think that the first book that belongs to them is the Bible—the Word of God—is an indescribable gift that will keep giving. When possible, our international partners arrange to have a ceremony, with little caps and gowns. For children who likely will never go through the formality of a school graduation, this is monumental for them. Some reports indicate that 46 percent of the world's population is not educated. For parents to witness their children being commended for the study of God's Word through this program is bearing fruit.

Many people do not comprehend the untold number of languages in the world. North of Australia, for example, the island nation of Papua New Guinea has over eight hundred tribal languages—more than any other country. However, most people understand a creole language called Tok Pisin. Since we have translated our materials into Tok Pisin, our church partners can use it to share the Gospel even in isolated communities that speak different languages and dialects.

The Greatest Journey is provided at no cost to the churches, giving them the opportunity to have an effective child evangelism ministry. Through this outreach, God is working all things together to draw an army of children to Him—children who represent the next generation of parents and spiritual leaders.

WATCH, FOR SALVATION IS NEAR

The thief never thought he'd go to church, but when he heard about the shoebox distribution he went to check it out. A shoebox distribution was being held at a church in San Ramon around the time I was holding an evangelistic festival in Montevideo, Uruguay, at Charrua Stadium.

Two brothers had gone to the church for the event and ran into a friend who had watched another boy steal the pastor's watch. They confronted him. The boy hung his head and confessed that he had done this hideous thing and went to the pastor and asked forgiveness.

The pastor accepted his apology and explained the importance of honesty in everything. He prayed with the little thief and then invited him to stay for the shoebox distribution. The boy couldn't believe that the pastor would let him receive a gift after what he had done, but he went.

Reluctant to accept the box he was handed, one of the volunteers told the boy that the gifts had come from Christians who wanted the children to know that Jesus loves them. He prodded the boy until he finally opened the box—inside was a watch. The boy left that day learning about confession that leads to forgiveness and forgiveness that leads to blessing.

God doesn't waste any circumstance in offering salvation to all.

"In the time of my favor I heard you, and in the day of salvation I helped you" (2 Cor. 6:2 NIV).

HAITI ROCKS

And that's just what Haiti needed following the massive 7.0 earthquake—salvation. This small island nation was rocked off its foundation in January 2010. The earth shook and then crumbled, killing three hundred thousand people. Millions were left homeless, injured and hopeless. They have had more than their share of misery.

Samaritan's Purse launched the largest emergency response in our more than forty-year history, providing medical care, food, water, and shelter for over five hundred thousand people.

Operation Christmas Child was a unique part of that response. Shoeboxes were shipped to Haiti for distribution through our local church partners. Greta Van Susteren and her husband John Coale had joined me to hand out boxes and Gospel booklets to more than one thousand children at a church in the slums of Cite Soleil.

We toured the epicenter of the catastrophic earthquake that rocked Haiti, and it was staggering to see the destruction in Leogane, where buildings and an orphanage were destroyed.

But it wasn't only the earthquake that had left Haitians in ruins. Ten months after Haiti rocked, a cholera epidemic migrated into the beleaguered island through United Nations peacekeepers, some from Nepal. Thousands of Haitians lost their lives, with thousands more at death's door.

Samaritan's Purse, already onsite, set up a medical response center where as many as twenty-three thousand had sought medical refuge, many of them children. However, we were in desperate need of an IV solution called Ringer's Lactate. The United States government had sent ample supply to Haiti, but the Haitian government was sitting on it while their people died.

I had appeared frequently as a guest of Fox News anchor Greta Van Susteren's "On the Record." Greta and her husband have great big hearts for the hurting, and for children around the world who are victims of poverty, homelessness, and anything that assaults the innocence of a child. Greta was amazed by the commitment of those who serve with our ministries and was always asking, "How can I help?"

So I called Greta and told her why treatment for patients in Haiti was moving slowly; not only for Samaritan's Purse, but for every other agency working there. She invited me to appear on her program that night, so I left for Washington. The next day we had Ringer's Lactate.

Greta gave us incalculable media coverage. She meant what she had said when she offered to help us, and proved it when she devoted a full hour of her nightly program to the relief work we were doing among the Haitian people in Jesus' name.

"People are in great need," Greta told the audience. "Sometimes you think this is horrible, tragic, very difficult, and hopeless, and then you run into the Samaritan's Purse people—volunteers and others who are bending over backwards, in this horrible heat, 24/7, giving up their lives to save these lives. You feel inspired."

Greta has been a great encouragement to our work. She and John have traveled with me to many parts of the world and Greta has given our ministry tremendous coverage on her program.

Former Governor Sarah Palin, her husband Todd, and daughter Bristol also traveled with us to Haiti to see the work at the cholera clinic, and helped us with a shoebox distribution. I had invited the Palins to fly with me to Haiti. I always caution my passengers not to board with tons of luggage, so I suggested they "pack light." Well, the Palins accustomed to flying in their Super Cub in the Alaska tundra, had no problem with that, but I was even astounded when they approached the plane—all three of them boarded with one backpack. I laughed and told them they could have fit all of that in a simple shoebox.

They were a delight to have with us and the Governor was in her element; she was great with the kids—holding them, hugging them—just thrilled to be there. We are always thankful to have people who are willing to set aside their busy schedules to come and help us and, as always, the children who receive the shoeboxes are the ones who ultimately bless our hearts with their smiles, their hugs, and their *mesi* (thank you).

God's love has been demonstrated in Haiti. "He alone is my rock and my salvation; he is my fortress, I will never be shaken" (Ps 62:2 NIV).

THE JOURNEY OF ONE
FOR THE SAVING OF ONE

I magine a little one receiving a soft bear to hug when just the night before he longed for security? Or a child grieved beyond description after watching her parents murdered; then she is given a little lamb that softly plays "Jesus Loves Me," finally lulling her to sleep? Or a young boy who is plagued with the horrific memories of violence that left him blinded, yet finds solace in music that comes through the headset of a Walkman? It's the simple things.

Most children in the West take simple things for granted. They loathe having to brush their teeth, while children living in squalor latch on to toothpaste and brush that brings refreshing delight—a necessity they seldom have. Our children and grandchildren may change their clothes multiple times a day; yet, entire families count themselves fortunate to have one set of clothes. If they get washed at all it would likely be in diseased water. To receive a brand new shirt, a soap bar, and a hair comb turns a hopeless kid into one that suddenly feels ten feet tall. It's the simple things.

Our purpose is not to just bring toys to children, just as Samaritan's Purse does not provide clean water, food parcels, medicines and shelter for physical needs only, but rather uses them to earn the privilege of telling others about God's salvation through His Son.

We cannot clothe everyone in need or feed all those who are hungry. We cannot provide clean drinking water to all villages. But the message we carry has the potential to clothe the lost with salvation.

The Bible says, "My soul shall be joyful in my God; for He has clothed me with the garments of salvation" (Isa. 61:10).

"If you extend your soul to the hungry and satisfy the afflicted soul, then your light shall dawn in the darkness, and your darkness shall be as the noonday" (Isa 58:10).

"As cold water to a weary soul, so is good news from a far country" (Prov. 25:25).

These simple shoebox gifts carry the Good News into far-away lands, into one heart at a time. That is the mission of Operation Christmas Child.

By going into these forsaken places, the seed of the Gospel is planted in hearts—many that are longing for God's truth, needing someone to tell them that truth is found in the Savior. To these hungry, thirsty, and sick souls the Scripture says, "Pleasant words are like a honeycomb, sweetness to the soul and health to the bones" (Prov. 16:24).

Yes, we want to take the pleasant words, forgiving words, and life-changing words of Jesus into these dark places; for He is the very Word that heals and saves.

I like to recall the story of Philip—the very first missionary named in Scripture and the very first to be called an evangelist. "Now an angel of the Lord spoke to Philip, saying, 'Arise and go toward the south along the road which goes down from Jerusalem to Gaza. This is desert'" (Acts 8:26).

Why the desert? There's little to no population in the desert. Philip had been preaching Christ among the people in Samaria—an extremely populated city filled with both Jews and Gentiles. The Holy Spirit was moving in the people's hearts and "multitudes with one accord heeded the things spoken by Philip" (Acts 8:6). There were great results from Philip's ministry. Why would the Lord command Philip to leave a thriving work and send him to the desert?

For one.

Philip "arose and went." Along the way he encountered an Ethiopian man who was sitting in his chariot reading Isaiah. Philip ran to him and said, "Do you understand what you are reading? And [the man] said, 'How can I, unless someone guides me?'" (Acts 8:30–31).

Then Philip "opened his mouth, and beginning at this Scripture, preached Jesus to him" (Acts 8:35).

This one man's belief in the claims of God's Son was so complete, that Philip baptized him in the water along the way.

Orphanages, hospitals, and far-away villages are deserts filled with parched hearts. Even a large city can be, to many, a dark and barren land. How can they hear about Jesus unless we tell them?

FROM THE BOX TO THE BIBLE

This was the frustration of Pastor Waisea in the South Pacific island of Fiji. He lives among a people surrounded by tropical beauty and spiritual darkness. But when our team in Australia heard his story about ten-year-old Ravi, they knew a spiritual breakthrough had taken place.

This Fijian pastor, who serves with OCC as one of our trainers and teachers, had long been praying for an opportunity to take the Gospel into the village of Vocalevu where there was no evangelical church. Operation Christmas Child sent shoeboxes to this area and of the eighty boxes distributed in this small village, thirty kids were enrolled for *The Greatest Journey.* Several children gave their hearts to Jesus—Ravi was one of them.

Because Ravi lived with his grandmother and grandfather, a tribal priest and the village witch doctor, they too began going through the Bible lessons with their grandson and the grandparents soon accepted Christ. In spite of the age difference, these new believers began the greatest journey together—walking with Jesus daily.

Ravi's grandfather began to grow in his faith and persuaded Pastor Waisea to use his home to start a church with twenty-five people. He then approached a landowner who sold him a quarter acre of land next to his home to build a small structure as a place of worship. Within a few months, this little group of believers that had swelled to forty began holding services on the land that would become the foundation of their church building.

From the box to the Bible, the Lord touched the heart of young Ravi who became an evangelist by sharing his faith with friends and family—even his grandfather. Ravi and his grandparents traded the worship of many gods for worshiping the one true God.

Our Australia office has reported that there are plans to help with the building of the church expected to be completed by the end of 2013, with a second church also being planted in a nearby village.

AJAY'S SIGHT MAGNIFIED

You could feel the excitement in the air! During a distribution in Fiji, one of our Australian volunteers was in the middle of a church filled with hundreds of young children eagerly waiting to get their boxes.

It was quite a scene as each child ripped open their box to discover the treasures inside. That is, each child except a little boy named Ajay. He sat at the end of a bench with his head down, hands in his lap.

Judy soon learned that Ajay was almost blind. His mom had recently died and Ajay had a lot to be sad about. When Judy sat down beside Ajay to help him open his shoebox, tears filled her eyes when she lifted the lid. The first thing visible was a magnifying glass. Judy knew that God had guided the gift-giver as the box was packed months before.

Lifting the magnifier, Judy held it up to *The Greatest Gift* booklet in front of Ajay's eyes. A smile crept across Ajay's face as he saw the colorful pages of the book and read the words that Jesus loves him.

Ajay, a calm boy, showed his delight when he held the magnifying glass up to Judy and said, *"vinaka"* (thank you). When the event was over, Ajay said a gentle good-bye, squeezing Judy's hand. It was a simple, yet profound expression of thanks from a child whose whole world was opened up through the power of a simple gift, sent with love from a stranger who cared and followed the leading of a still small voice.

The power and gentleness of the still small voice from Heaven speaks to millions of packers who are listening to God's prompting in such a simple but profound way, and is the same voice that whispers to recipients "Come." "O magnify the Lord with me" (Ps. 34:3).

THIS LITTLE SPARK

G uyana! When my daughter Cissie told me she was going there, I was thrilled to see Samaritan's Purse reaching out to the people of that small South American nation. I had visited that nation's infamous Jonestown a few years after the horrific 1978 massacre, led by cult leader Jim Jones. It was good to know that in Guyana—in the twenty-first century—the name of the Lord Jesus Christ was being lifted up and glorified through Operation Christmas Child.

Joseph Barker, a full-time OCC volunteer, was Cissie's Guyanese host and, along with our video crew, they traveled by canoe to visit Santa Mission along the Kamuni River, winding beneath the jungle canopy.

Cissie captured an eyewitness account of the picturesque landscape surrounded by extreme poverty. But the smiles on children's faces were the evidence that they were rich, not poor. Many still carried around their shoebox gifts from a distribution that had been done earlier. When Cissie walked into a classroom to actually teach a lesson from *The Greatest Journey*, the children's eyes lit up knowing they were going to learn more that day about Jesus. Before her visit ended, Cissie had the opportunity to present personalized certificates to each of the graduates. "Then to give them a Bible," Cissie said, "meant more to them than anything they had received."

When she got back to the States she called to tell me what she had seen and heard and what most impacted her heart. "Dad," she said, "this is an incredible program! Working through the local church, like Samaritan's Purse has always done, gives these pastors a way to reach children through the literature that follows the boxes. This is the long-term spiritual effect that OCC is having on these communities and on the young generation. The spark has been lit in these churches and this is just the beginning!"

Cissie went on to tell me how effective Joseph was as he also led the children in a lesson or two. "Dad," Cissie said, "Joseph told the kids what I remember hearing in Sunday school, 'You can't light a candle and put it under a bushel; you put it on a stand for the world to see. Where there is a change in a person's life, it cannot be hidden.'"

Boy Shepherd Hears
The Great Shepherd

J ust twenty years ago, it would have been illegal to go to Sunday school and learn about Jesus in Communist countries. In fact, any religion was strictly forbidden during nearly seventy years of Soviet rule.

But with the collapse of the Communist regime in 1990, doors to the Gospel began to open in Mongolia, a vast and sparsely populated nation between China and Russia. Still, missionaries found church planting to be a difficult task as cultural religions took root in the culture.

We began sending shoebox gifts to Mongolia in 1996 where we had led a series of relief and evangelism projects. Our Children's Heart Project helped save the lives of over two hundred and sixty children in Mongolia who were born with heart defects.

"Mongolians think Christianity is a foreign religion," wrote Moujic Baatar, national leadership team member, "but when we distribute shoeboxes and tell people about God's love, that really touches their hearts. The boxes show that God is not asking them to do something for Him and He is not angry with them. This is a very different God than what they are taught in their religion."

Today there are several hundred churches in the country, and about two percent of the population of three million consider themselves Christians.

Through the project, children and their families who live in some of the most remote provinces of Mongolia are being reached with the Gospel. One of these children is Balginyan, a teenager who received a shoebox gift last year in the mountain community of Ulzit.

Balginyan rises early every morning to milk his family's cows and helps his father look after their herd of sheep, goats, and yaks. Horses are his mode of transportation as he leads the livestock to good pasture.

When the boy opened his box, he was amazed to find a beautiful toy horse, as well as other small gifts. Along with his box, Balginyan also received *The Greatest Gift of All* booklet in his own language. So taken by the story and pictures, Balginyan carried it with him when he herded the sheep that evening.

"I took the book with me and read it," he said. "After that, I started to read the Bible and I began to pray. I learned that God is a shepherd, the Great Shepherd."

As thousands of Mongolian children receive shoebox gifts, they are also hearing the blessed news of the Good Shepherd who lovingly cares for His flock.

Jesus said, "I am the gate; whoever enters through me will be saved. He will come in and go out, and find pasture. The thief comes only to steal and kill and destroy; I have come that they may have life, and have it to the full" (John 10:9–10 NIV).

Bringing Light to a Mountain Village

Melvin Perez wanted to take gifts to the children in the mountain village of El Picacho, Honduras, with a population of fifteen hundred people. It's a four-hour hike from the nearest road. Visitors are rare, but all the more reason for a Samaritan's Purse visit. We love to find these places because it gives us a chance to tell people that they aren't forgotten. It was, however, an exhausting trip that required the team members to hoist cartons of gifts on their shoulders as they climbed the rocky path.

But when two hundred and seventy-five children gathered in school to receive their gifts—the hard trip had been worth the effort. Parents watched with delight as children opened gifts, finding toys, school supplies, and basic necessities. Flashlights were especially popular because El Picacho has no electricity.

One community leader was so moved by the Christmas message, the gifts, and the effort made to deliver them, that he offered a large tract of his own land to build the first church in El Picacho. People were excited about the prospect until they realized that construction supplies must be hauled on shoulders or mules in the same grueling fashion as the shoeboxes came up. But Melvin, one of our project leaders, knew this was the crowning blessing of the shoebox ministry—to plant a church and win the lost. He and his team have been faithful to return.

As the word has spread of what God is doing in El Picacho, other communities have asked Melvin's group to come share the Gospel and help them plant churches. "Now the Gospel is moving in seven different communities," Melvin said with joy. "And it all started with two hundred and seventy-five shoeboxes."

"All over the world this gospel is bearing fruit and growing, just as it has been doing among you since the day you heard it and understood God's grace in all its truth" (Col. 1:6 NIV).

WITCH DOCTORS GO ON THE GREATEST JOURNEY

This is something Lucia was about to learn—God's grace in all its truth—which was very different from what he had been taught.

"My grandparents were the witch doctors of my village," his letter started out.

I am Lucia and I live in Chiriqui, Panama. One day I was invited to a children's program sponsored by Samaritan's Purse and they gave me shoebox. I had never had one before. They told us to come back the next Saturday for another program, but my mom wouldn't let me go. I cried so much that she finally gave in. When I arrived with some other children, we were given some Bible lessons, but I couldn't read too well. They told me to take it home and maybe my mother would help me read.

When she saw what it was, she was afraid to read them. She had always been told that if we read the Bible we would die. I was so disappointed. But as she thought about how happy the shoebox gift had made me, she started reading the book to me when my dad was away at work so no one would know. We went through many lessons and were surprised that nothing bad happened to us. The book told us how we could receive Jesus in our hearts, and we prayed to Him to forgive us, and Christ accepted us as His children.

My dad and brother started reading the book and we began going to church as a family. We were surprised when my grandparents began looking through the material and now they no longer practice witchcraft. Thank you for giving this to me and please keep giving it to all the children who get shoebox gifts. It's the best part of the gift and my family is proof.

A shoebox isn't sent forth without prayer and the Lord is hearing, answering, and blessing those who are faithful.

SQUEALING FOR A CHURCH

U nder the jackfruit trees in the Filipino village of Indang, two hours outside Manila, he watched as a church was planted in the hearts of little believers. The small group of children who had received shoebox gifts had started meeting under the trees, but their smiles would turn to frowns when it rained, as it often does in the Philippines.

This was the result of the discipleship course that followed the shoebox gifts in 2011. Discouraged by the rain, the thirty-five boys and fifty-nine girls approached Helen Plagata, who spearheads the outreach and teaches the lessons, about whether God could provide a church building for them.

Moved greatly by such a request from those so young, Helen knew this was a teaching moment for them in faith. "Why don't you pray about it and ask God for a church," Helen encouraged them, believing that God's heart would be touched by the children's desire to meet together in His name.

They accepted the challenge. The man in the village who had been watching the children meet to study the Bible, even in the downpours, was touched by God to donate a small parcel of land.

The kids squealed with joy upon hearing the news. Adults and children gathered bamboo, and a ten-foot-square-meter nipa hut was erected. The little church was dedicated in 2012. Four benches and a pulpit fit nicely under the roof—as do the children.

Children's lives are being transformed and added to Christ's church.

MISTER, THERE'S SOMETHING WRONG . . .

Hardly a week passes that we don't hear another story about a soul being saved, a church being planted, and a home being mended because a shoebox opened a door. But sometimes we receive stories that make our hearts skip a beat when things don't go exactly right; yet in the end, it seems the Lord turns it right side up.

One of our African partners working with our team in the United Kingdom told about a young boy who approached him during a shoebox distribution with these words, "Mister, there's something wrong."

"My heart skipped a beat," the man said. "Standing in front of me was a child, nine or ten. Then he told the whole story."

"The children had gathered on a grassy bank which sloped sharply into the lake. Those helping were concerned that if the children got too excited when the gifts were presented, there could be shoving and pushing. We were afraid some might end up in the lake with the crocodiles, hippos and us!"

"In an effort to keep them calm and easy to handle, we got the children singing. Such volume and harmony!" But when the distribution began, the calm and gentle sounds were blasted away by the whoops and hollers that skipped like stones across the water. The hillside had come alive.

The man headed up the hill to capture the moment on film. That's when the boy ran up to him and said, "Mister, there's something wrong," as he held up a tin in one hand and the shoebox in the other.

"'Lord, help me,' I prayed, not sure I was equipped to handle the problem. Distress was written all over his face. I bent down to look him in the eyes and he shoved an empty tin toward me. I knew in Swaziland that people thought it bad luck to give an empty purse—an empty anything—as a gift without at least putting a coin inside. Here was this little boy with an empty tin. I was thinking shoeboxes, not tins. The boy was so distraught. It wasn't that he was ungrateful for the box full of other gifts; he simply could not understand the empty container that had come inside the box."

The boy's eyes looked perplexed. The man breathed a sigh of helplessness, until he remembered that shoeboxes are about communicating God's love. So the man engaged him in conversation and found out that the boy had hoped to bring his little sister a gift, but there were only enough shoeboxes for those in attendance.

Prayer was answered. The man took the tin and explained to the boy how wonderful the people had been to pack the box with enough things for two children—the boy and his sister. The man proceeded to show the boy how he could make two gifts out of one, and cautiously took duplicate items like pencils, balloons, candy, and stickers, and filled the tin full for his sister. The boy looked into the tin, then down to his box. As a smile replaced the frown marks on his face, his little hand reached into the box and added a few more choice gifts that would fit into the tin.

The man said to the boy, "You must love your sister very much to give her so much of your gift." The boy shook his head. The man tenderly put his arm around the young boy and told him that Jesus loved him, too, and wanted to give him a gift. The boy smiled and hugged the gifts and the storybook, then ran up the hill toward home.

While we may never know how God works in the lives of those children, we can be sure that the Gospel was presented and exemplified through a loving touch and a caring heart.

A Sermon Written with Ink, about a Love Written in Blood

From Swaziland to Kenya, we are always blessed to hear from pastors and our church partners.

Had it not been for *The Greatest Journey* discipleship course, children in Nakuru, Kenya, may have never heard that God loves them and wants to save them from sin. They may have never known that they could be His disciples and live to tell others about the greatest gift that has ever been given to the world—His name is Jesus.

My son Will (who serves with the BGEA as Vice President of The Billy Graham Training Center at The Cove in Asheville, North Carolina) was preaching an evangelistic meeting (called a "celebration") in Nakuru, Kenya. During the several day meeting, he took time to lead an Operation Christmas Child shoebox distribution at a nearby school. Children assembled there not only received beautiful gifts but they learned about Jesus that day. Then they were invited to participate in our follow-up discipleship course, giving them the opportunity to turn their lives over to the Lord and live in obedience to Him.

Year after year we hear of our Bible-study curriculum having an impact not only on children, but their parents. When moms and dads see the change in their children's lives, they have to consider why. The answer lies within the pages of *The Greatest Journey*, which points students to the Bible. Pastors and teachers give witness to the fact that the Word of God makes a difference.

A pastor/father wrote, describing a Christmas they would never forget.

My church was the blessed recipient of your generosity when you came to Nakuru, Kenya, with bright packages of love for our children. And may I say to you, dear sisters and brothers, that without the pen used to write this letter, I would be unable to convey my deep gratitude and thanks.

You see, my son received a shoebox. How precious of him to go through the box of toys and find something to give me—an ink pen—because his father writes sermons to preach. I am so grateful that while the children treasure their gifts, they all have tried to give to others out of their great joy. That's the sermon I'll preach soon, that Jesus gave out of His joy and wrote His letter of love on the cross with His blood.

"Asante" (thank you) to the children, families, and churches who have given out of their joy to spread God's love all the way here to us in the heart of Africa. The boxes you have sent are a blessing to us.

I Wanna Go Hand Out Shoeboxes!

That's exactly what Sean Hannity, FOX News anchor said to me "on the air live," shortly before Christmas 2011.

For years, Sean has invited me to appear on his program *Hannity*, not to talk about politics, but to talk about the world's largest international Christmas program for children—Operation Christmas Child.

Every December, I fly to New York armed with one thing—a shoebox. When the cameras come on and Sean welcomes me, he wants to know about OCC and where we're going that Christmas. As he interviews me about the project he unpacks the box, often playing with different toys. So when he said on the air that he wanted to go on one of these distributions, I told him I'd love it. But sometimes people show excitement out of politeness. I waited until after the program and then queried him, "Are you really serious about going on a shoebox distribution?"

"Yep, and Jill and I would love to take our kids."

Sean and his wife Jill have been donors to Samaritan's Purse for some time. I knew he had a heart for kids, so right after Christmas, I flew to Florida where they were vacationing and picked them up and took them with me to the Dominican Republic.

Jill is an Alabama country girl and she was wonderful with the kids assembled there waiting for their gifts. Their own children, Patrick and Merri Kelly, are polite and inquisitive. They really got into the moment and were fabulous with the little ones. They worked hard but took time to play with the children, explaining how different toys worked. Sean is kind of a big kid himself. While many think of him only as "thick-skinned," Sean has a tender heart. He sat on the ground and let the kids crawl all over him as he helped them unpack their boxes—he had them giggling and talking.

Scotty McCreary, the 2011 *American Idol* winner, was with us. He and his family had packed shoeboxes for years. He's been a big help to us just getting others excited about OCC. He traveled to churches and schools singing to the children, playing with them, and praying for them. He hit it off with the Hannity kids and it was evident that Christmas for kids in the Dominican Republic was a big hit for them too!

PERSECUTED THEN PROTECTED

Church members were ruthlessly persecuted by their neighbors in a town on the outskirts of a Mexican city. The small evangelical church was assaulted time and again: windows broken, graffiti painted on the walls, and garbage dumped on church property.

The church was concerned for their own protection and the structure they had worked so hard to build. They thought of ways to retaliate—to protect what was rightfully theirs. When they began to pray, asking God what they could do to stop the ill will toward them, an unusual answer came in the form of shoeboxes.

Operation Christmas Child was making arrangements to hold a distribution in the area and asked the church how many boxes they could use. As church leaders and parents debated how to best use the boxes for the sake of the Gospel, the message grabbed hold of their hearts. "Love your neighbor as yourself" (Mark 12:31).

"We will give the boxes to the children of our neighbors who are persecuting us." And that is exactly what they did. The church extended an invitation to their enemies to "come to church with your children; we have gifts for them."

The persecutors brought their children out of curiosity, some said later. Parents were speechless to watch the children of the church give shoebox gifts to their children. Afterward, refreshments were served and the church families greeted their guests with hugs, smiles, and words of truth from the Bible. From that time on, the hostile neighbors became the church's protectors, and some have even stepped across the threshold of hostility into the peace of

God's love. "When a man's ways please the LORD, he makes even his enemies to be at peace with him" (Prov. 16:7).

We have seen this happen in countries around the world—in communities that harbored hostilities—but the shoeboxes have exemplified God's peace, bringing reconciliation and nourishment to the soul. God's Word breaks down barriers.

Spiritual Hunger in Hungary

Famines plague many nations. The word *famine* means "the acute shortage of anything." While there are famines of food and water, the greatest famine is that of the Word of God.

"Behold, the days are coming," says the Lord GOD, "that I will send a famine on the land, not a famine of bread, nor a thirst for water, but of hearing the words of the LORD" (Amos 8:11).

People are hungry for truth; they just don't know where to find it. In Hungary, however, churches—our ministry partners—are rejoicing as children respond to the Word of God through the shoebox ministry and evangelism materials.

"We wish to thank the brethren for their financial sacrifice that made it possible to allow such a large gathering of people to hear of our faith," a pastor wrote. "It brought such joy." But after all the gifts had been handed out, a woman with two children came by and saw all the activity inside the church, and she asked to come in.

The pastor explained what had taken place and expressed sorrow that there were no more gifts to offer her children. She said, "We heard the beautiful songs, the readings and the harmony of the presenters. The joy I received is my gift, *'koszonom'* (I thank you)."

It was the pastor who felt he had received a special gift when he heard the woman say that she understood the message: that Jesus came to earth as a Babe and was King of the world and Lord of the heart.

"There will be another collection someday," he said, "when He comes back to gather the redeemed." The pastor called upon all to open their hearts to Jesus and find forgiveness that brings joy. "We are most grateful that it was not just the result of happy children with boxes," the pastor wrote, "but serious decisions made in hearts to receive the greatest gift found in the Lord Jesus. If only I could, I would gladly condense the shrieks and shouts of joy of ten thousand children and the sight of their expecting eyes into one single letter."

From Deadly Spears to God's Carvings

※

Uno, dos, tres: Abran sus cajas (one, two, three: Open your boxes)! Wild excitement sweeps across the schoolyard as two hundred and fifty boys and girls launch into opening their shoeboxes as fast as they can. Operation Christmas Child has come to Ecuador.

This is the town of Shell, on the edge of the Amazon jungle. But for the villagers today, looking forward does not mean they don't look back.

An elderly couple, with distinctive facial features of the Waorani Indians, smile as they watch their grandson hold up a toy he's just pulled out of his shoebox. A plane from Mission Aviation Fellowship (MAF) airport, some three hundred yards away, lifts off and glides past the jubilant gathering. The old man, Mincaye, glances up briefly at the plane, remembering.

It was a day that went down in history fifty-seven years ago. On a Sunday afternoon in January 1956, five missionaries from the United States were ambushed and killed by Waorani Indians whom they had come to befriend and to tell about the love of Jesus. Mincaye was one of the warriors who attacked the missionaries that day on a river sandbar in the jungle. He speared to death thirty-two-year-old Nate Saint, the MAF pilot who flew the missionaries into the jungle from the same Shell airbase. The tribesman had felt threatened by the foreigners and their strange aircraft the Indians described as a "wood bee." It wasn't until Saint's sister, Rachel, and Jim Elliot's widow, Elisabeth, came to live with the Waorani two years later that Mincaye heard the Gospel—which he still describes as "God's carvings."

"I grew up in a place where no one ever talked about there being a God," Mincaye said. "I didn't know His carvings [writings]. All I knew was violence and killing. If I didn't kill people, they would kill me."

His attitude reflected the feelings of the Chinese people when my grandfather went to China to serve its people—they said he was a foreign devil in China. But the Waorani tribe learned, as did the Chinese people, that God's servants did not come to take life, but to bring a life-saving message.

That's when Mincaye's life, and heart, began to change. The fierce warrior, who was as fearless as a lion, became convicted as he sought to know the love and grace of God. "I was filled with a joy I had never experienced before. I left the life of violence behind and decided to continue the work of the missionaries by sharing the Gospel with my people," he said.

A half century later, Mincaye has traveled far beyond the Amazon basin to tell others about the Savior. He has been to the United States and across the ocean to Europe and Asia. He and his family now partner with us in the ministry of OCC.

Shoeboxes have been distributed in Ecuador since 2001, but until 2008 they had never been delivered to children in the remote jungle east of the Andes Mountains. Mincaye and his wife, Umpura, wanted to participate in this once-in-a-lifetime event. They were even more excited when they learned that their great-grandchildren would be receiving shoebox gifts.

Mincaye joined in the fun with Inehue, age five, and Nicole, age eight, as they pulled out some of the treasures in their boxes. Mincaye's grandson Gilberto wants other children to experience the blessings his children received; he works with a missionary group that recently led a shoebox distribution deep into the jungle, to Indian villages unreached with the Gospel. "The missionaries came here in 1956 so we could have the Bible and know God," he said. "Now through the shoeboxes, we have a tool to share the Gospel with children in remote villages and to minister to their parents."

The missionaries and pilot did not die in vain. Many in that village came to know Christ and in 1966, Nate Saint's children, Steve and Kathy, were baptized in the Curaray River by two of the men who had killed their father. In 1995, Steve and his family returned to Ecuador to continue the ministry their mother, Rachel, had for decades among the Waorani.

The story lives on, demonstrating forgiveness that comes only from the Lord. Mincaye adopted Nate Saint's grandchildren as his own and they enjoy the sweet fellowship of the "saints."

When the Billy Graham Evangelistic Association held an itinerant evangelism conference in Amsterdam in 2000, we were privileged to have Steve Saint speak to national church leaders. Mincaye was there with him and gave his testimony to the eleven thousand that filled the arena as Steve stood by his side and translated for him.

"My ancestors lived angry, hating each other," Mincaye said. "Whenever foreigners came into our land, we would just spear them. We didn't know God's carvings. How could we walk God's trail if we didn't see God's carvings? When I killed Steve's father, I did not know any better. We didn't know he was coming to teach us of God's trail."

The movie *End of the Spear*, based on Steve Saint's book by the same name, premiered in 2006, fifty years after the attack. Two years later, in 2008, it was remarkable to witness Mincaye and Umpura as they watched their grandson Gilberto and his family experience the joy of receiving shoebox gifts given in the name of Jesus.

It is only by God's grace and His forgiveness that men, women, and children can be set free from the guilt and pain of sin. It is because Christ forgives that we can forgive and experience the joy of salvation found in such a Savior.

FIRSTS

We were fast approaching the twentieth anniversary of Operation Christmas Child. As 2012 progressed and OCC season neared, we knew by Christmastime we would collect our one hundred millionth shoebox.

How do we celebrate something of this magnitude? The answer came quickly: by not forgetting what God had done. By remembering how He had laid the foundation and gave us the building blocks of prayer, faith, and obedience, moved us upward and onward. We wanted to thank Him for the past and thank Him for what He still had in store—one hundred million was just the beginning!

We wanted to do something special to highlight the one hundred millionth shoebox soon to be collected. The OCC team identified Evilyn Pinnow from Wisconsin to pack the special shoebox. Serving as our child spokesperson in 2012, Evilyn appeared at each of our press conferences. With her mother, Evilyn visited California, Tennessee, New York, Colorado, and Minnesota, adding special items from people whose lives had been touched by OCC.

There are so many children that could have been chosen for this special assignment; countless children have collected and wrapped gifts with the motivation to use them to share God's love for others.

But Evilyn came to mind because she had been packing gift boxes for kids, and with kids, in a unique and creative way. At eight years old, she started her own Shoebox Club with friends in Fort Atkinson, Wisconsin. At twelve years old, there are now over eighty members meeting each month with over two thousand shoeboxes packed. This is remarkable for children so young.

Evilyn represented the hearts of all OCC children well as she prepared to deliver this shoebox. When the last items filled the box, it was sealed and prayed over at our press conference in Charlotte, North Carolina, and Evilyn and her mother traveled with our distribution team to the Dominican Republic to make a very special delivery.

THE HUNDRED MILLIONTH SHOEBOX

The shoebox was wrapped in white paper covered with red, green, blue and yellow handprints. The lid was slightly humped because the contents spilled over with sunglasses, a jump rope, art supplies, clothes, and costume jewelry. But the recipient especially loved the cuddly lamb.

Little Brenda Valdez was the child chosen to receive the symbolic one hundred millionth shoebox. It seemed fitting since she herself had been put down in a box when she was just months old and delivered to her father's aunt. Her story touched our hearts.

Brenda had been born to an unwed mother in the Dominican Republic and neglected. The mother did not want her and the father was not able to care for her. Desperate for her well-being, he gave her to his aunt, Christiana Guzman, who lives in a rural community not far from Santa Domingo, the capital of the Caribbean nation.

Five years later, Brenda is healthy and full of life. Like any child, she loves presents. Perhaps that's why she couldn't stop smiling, her pink tongue poking through the space for her two missing front teeth, when Evilyn handed her the symbolic one hundred millionth shoebox in December 2012.

Brenda's gift box is among over 2.2 million handed out in the Dominican Republic since 1999. In a nation of nine million people, that's enough to reach an entire generation with the transforming power of the Gospel.

Pastor Fidel Lorenzo said as many as twelve churches are planted across the Dominican Republic each year as a direct result of shoebox distributions. "The Dominican Republic is at the perfect moment to change the next generation," he said, "and OCC is the perfect instrument that will allow us to make this change."

A Christmas to Remember

E cuador sits on the symbolic line that divides the earth in half with twelve-hour periods of daylight and darkness.

After Christmas 2012, I took my oldest grandchild CJ (age twelve), to Ecuador for her first shoebox distribution. Traveling with us was Michael W. Smith, his wife Debbie, and her mother Ann, and Patti (Michael and Debbie's daughter-in-law).

We had just celebrated Christmas in our homes so it was a special treat to celebrate Christmas all over again with the beautiful children of this South American nation.

The Smiths jumped right into the fun helping children open their boxes and showing them the love of the One the Christmas season celebrates.

CJ is very much like my son Will; she made friends easily and was excited to watch the children gasp with surprise, giggle with delight, and grab hold of their precious gift boxes. She sat with some of the children as they combed through the presents, sometimes showing them how to use certain things.

Then a little girl pulled out a picture of a family and showed it to CJ. Her mouth dropped open. It was a picture of the family who had packed the box—a family that CJ knew well.

This has happened on occasion with various team members who travel with OCC, and it is always a fun moment, but it is also evidence that God's guides. What other explanation could be made that this one box, out of nine million collected for that year, would have come from people CJ knew? It thrilled me that she was able to see God at work; for my granddaughter, it made her first distribution a Christmas to remember.

A Hundred Million Reasons
to Celebrate ✳

The twentieth anniversary of Operation Christmas Child is nothing short of a miracle from Heaven. As our teams returned from all over the world after Christmas 2012, stories poured in declaring what had been done through the power of simple gifts in Jesus' name.

In April 2013 in Orlando, Florida, Samaritan's Purse held a great celebration to give glory to God for using Operation Christmas Child to spread the Gospel abroad and to express thanks to the army of people who serve in His name. It was the culmination of the Global Connect Conference where three thousand volunteers from around the world gathered to fellowship and praise the Lord together for blessing multitudes of children who are not forgotten by God, and not forgotten by OCC.

This gala was a shining reflection of God's goodness. His miracle working power had placed one hundred million shoebox gifts into one hundred million pairs of hands. His Gospel seed carried by the boxes had been deposited into a hundred million hearts. God's Word, translated into eighty languages, had fallen into the hands of parents, government officials, witch doctors, and medicine men. That seed today is producing souls for His kingdom.

As ten thousand volunteers and donors from one hundred and two nations gathered at the Orange County Convention Center and the evening was opened in prayer led by Dr. Ross Rhoads, praise was lifted beyond the rafters and into Heaven.

Our hearts were moved—sometimes to tears—to hear from our full circle kids who had miraculously accepted Jesus Christ after receiving a simple shoebox gift and hearing the Gospel story about the Christmas Child who gave the Greatest Gift of all—Himself—as the Savior who saves sinners. These kids, no longer children, have learned what it means to embark on *The Greatest Journey* with Christ and follow in His steps.

Ricky Skaggs and Dennis Agajanian were on stage with their guitars, playing and singing as they had done for twenty years at OCC events. The Tommy Coomes Band also took the platform and delighted the crowd by singing in multiple languages: Russian, Arabic, Spanish, and Portuguese—as they had done from the start. Matthew West did more than sing; he told of the many distributions he had done with OCC, delivering shoeboxes in far-away lands.

The African Children's Choir performed as a spectacular flag processional made its way down the aisles, representing every nation visited by Operation Christmas Child, and reminding us that "All the nations you have made will come and worship before you, O Lord; they will bring glory to your name. For you are great and do marvelous deeds . . ." (Ps. 86:9–10 NIV).

Michael W. Smith, who has made multiple trips with me and helped us in our ministries around the world, warmed the hearts of the people that night through his music and witness of how this children's evangelism program—using a simple shoebox—had affected him.

Then a hush fell over the arena after a standing ovation for our hillbilly angel, Mary Damron, who joined me on stage. Mary, with her trademark bare feet, reflected how she had been led to jump in feet first to "help God's children." With Dennis, Tommy, and Ricky, we reminisced about that first and most dangerous trek into Sarajevo eighteen years earlier. When I asked if Mary would sing "God on the Mountain," she readily agreed as long as all the guys would back her up.

Then, like the shoeboxes, we wrapped the evening in prayer as Rev. Sami Dagher led us to the throne of the great God we serve, thanking Him for leading, guiding, and answering prayer for the salvation of a multitude of children—for Jesus does call little children to Him.

The best way I know to end a book about Operation Christmas Child is to wrap it in this thought—

> When one hundred million prayers are lifted to Heaven
> for one hundred million boxes
> that will be given to one hundred million souls,
> might Jesus lean up on the edge of His throne and say—
> I have used these gifts given in My name
> To open the children's hearts
> And My offer remains to all who come seeking
> For I will answer.

This was a celebration for what God had done through Operation Christmas Child. But He's not done yet. *The Greatest Journey* has many more miles to travel and many more souls to reach—and we'll continue telling *A Story of Simple Gifts*.

AFTERWORD: WRITING A SIMPLE STORY

Are these stories worth telling? Broadman & Holman (B&H) Publishing Group (LifeWay) thought so. They came to Boone and challenged us to "write this simple story about simple gifts" as a way to celebrate the twentieth anniversary of Operation Christmas Child. We agreed.

Appreciative of the publisher's enthusiasm, we invited Selma Wilson, president of B&H Publishing Group and Jennifer Lyell, B&H Trade Book Publisher to travel with our distribution team to Peru in 2013. They were excited to meet the team hosted by Randy Riddle. Upon their return home, Selma wrote:

> I have watched from this side of the world the operation of OCC and have always been impressed with this ministry. But to see it lived out through the actual delivery of these shoeboxes was beyond anything expected.
>
> The operational excellence of the team was impressive with every detail planned out and executed so well. The volunteer team on the field in Peru was outstanding, and I loved that this ministry was done through churches. Each church visit was a celebration for the pastor and his team of leaders.
>
> After this memorable trip, our vision has grown about what the message of this book could mean for the advancement of the Gospel. I pray that through this publishing partnership, people will feel the tug to do more for the kingdom of God through OCC—let's pray that the one hundred million shoeboxes will double.

And this is our prayer also; not only that we'll see another one hundred million shoeboxes for kids, but that within five years we will put into the hands of these recipients *The Greatest Journey* Discipleship Course so that the Gospel can be used to deepen children's understanding of Scripture and build the next generation to "go" and tell what Jesus Christ has done for them.

SAMARITAN'S PURSE MISSION STATEMENT

S amaritan's Purse is a nondenominational evangelical Christian organization providing spiritual and physical aid to hurting people around the world. Since 1970, Samaritan's Purse has helped meet the needs of people who are victims of war, poverty, natural disasters, disease, and famine with the purpose of sharing God's love through His Son, Jesus Christ. The organization serves the church worldwide to promote the Gospel of the Lord Jesus Christ.

The mission of Operation Christmas Child is to demonstrate God's love in a tangible way to needy children around the world, and together with the local church worldwide, to share the Good News of Jesus Christ.

Samaritan's Purse International
P.O. Box 3000
Boone, NC 28607
Phone: 828.262.1980

Learn about more ways to participate in Operation Christian Child at: www.samaritanspurse.org
Facebook: www.facebook.com/OCCshoeboxes
Twitter: @OCC_shoeboxes

VOLUNTEER WITH OPERATION CHRISTMAS CHILD

More than one hundred thousand dedicated volunteers in the United States share the love of Jesus Christ and the joy of Christmas with millions of boys and girls. There are several ways you can partner with us:

MAKE THE BIGGEST IMPACT BY VOLUNTEERING YEAR-ROUND

In 2005, Operation Christmas Child was introduced to the biblically based High Impact Volunteer Recruitment, selection, training and multiplication principles and process. The project experienced a paradigm shift that changed the nature of mobilizing the body of Christ worldwide in OCC, more effectively connecting the follower of Jesus with their giftedness, calling, and service opportunity unto the Lord. At Operation Christmas Child, year-round volunteers, also known as "Connect Volunteers," serve on Area Teams to organize, promote, and pray for the ministry in their own area throughout the year and to facilitate shoebox gift collections. It is the key building block to deepen and expand the volunteer capacity and to encourage and facilitate unity in the body of Christ worldwide.

Dedicated volunteers work year-round to promote and pray for Operation Christmas Child. Teams of people are coming together around the country to serve in the specific areas of prayer, church relations, community relations, media relations, and shoebox collections. Opportunities are available to use your gifts in these areas.

Connect Conferences were created to further inspire, challenge, and equip OCC Connect volunteers. The first Connect Conference was held in 2007. In 2013, more than three thousand Connect volunteers from throughout the world (more than one hundred and twenty countries) attended the Global Connect Conference in Orlando. This historical Global Connect Conference allowed the key volunteer leaders to hear what God is doing among the nations and it allows us to sow encouragement into their hearts and express our appreciation for their extraordinary service to the Lord.

Learn more about becoming an OCC Connect volunteer at www.samaritanspurse.org.

SERVE AT A COLLECTION SITE DURING NATIONAL COLLECTION WEEK

An exciting way for groups and individuals to serve the Lord through Operation Christmas Child is to volunteer at one of our collection sites. Opportunities to volunteer are available during National Collection Week.

INSPECT AND PREPARE SHOEBOX GIFTS AT A PROCESSING CENTER

Millions of lives are touched by shoebox gifts collected each year. Each precious gift is carefully inspected and prepared for overseas shipment by caring people. Opportunities to volunteer in Processing Centers around the United States are available in November and December. Volunteers in the Processing Center must be at least thirteen years of age or older. Please visit our website for the latest information about signing up to serve at a Processing Center.

PARTICIPATE BY PACKING A SHOEBOX GIFT

Use an empty shoebox or a small plastic container. You can wrap the box (lid separately). Most important, pray for the child who will receive your gift.

Determine whether your gift will be for a boy or a girl, and the child's age category: 2-4, 5-9, or 10-14. Print out the appropriate boy/girl label by downloading the artwork on the website. Mark the correct age category on the label, and tape the label to the top of your box.

Fill the box with a variety of gifts that will bring delight to a child. Use the gift ideas provided on the bottom of this page. Please include "a key toy," at least one item a child can immediately embrace such as a stuffed toy, doll, ball, or toy truck.

Please donate $7 or more for each shoebox you prepare to help cover shipping and other project costs. You can give online by using our "Follow Your Box Donation" option, or you can write a check to Samaritan's Purse (note "OCC" on the memo line) and place it in an envelope on top of the gift items inside your box. If you or your family are preparing more than one shoebox, please make one combined donation.

Place a rubber band around each closed shoebox and drop it off at the collection center nearest you during our National Collection Week (refer to website annually). For locations and hours of collection visit our "Drop-Off Locations" page where you can find the nearest place to take your shoebox by entering your Zip Code or you can call 1-800-353-5949. You can also send your shoebox gift to: Samaritan's Purse/Operation Christmas Child, 801 Bamboo Road, Boone, NC 28607

SHOEBOX GIFT SUGGESTIONS

SCHOOL SUPPLIES: Pens, pencils and sharpeners, crayons or markers, stamps and ink pad sets, writing pads or paper, solar calculators, coloring and picture books, etc.

TOYS: Small cars, balls, dolls, stuffed animals, kazoos, harmonicas, yo-yos, jump ropes, small Etch A Sketch, toys that light up or make noise (with extra batteries), Slinky, etc.

HYGIENE ITEMS: Toothbrush, toothpaste, mild bar soap (in a plastic bag), comb, washcloth, etc.

OTHER: T-shirts, socks, ball caps, sunglasses, hair clips, toy jewelry, watches, flashlights (with extra batteries).

A PERSONAL NOTE: You may enclose a note to the child and a photo of yourself or your family. (If you include your name and address, the child may write back).

DO NOT INCLUDE: Used or damaged items; war-related items such as toy guns, knives or military figures; chocolate or food; out-of-date candy; liquids or lotions; medications or vitamins; breakable items such as snow globes or glass containers; aerosol cans.

FOLLOW YOUR BOX

Discover the ultimate destination of your Operation Christmas Child shoebox gift! By making your $7 donation online using a credit or debit card you will receive a special shoebox label included in your e-mail receipt. Print or copy the label as many times as you need to attach to each of your boxes.

Your specific barcode is connected to your e-mail address, so it's important to use the same label on each of your boxes. The barcode on the label enables us to track each shoebox gift. You will receive an e-mail telling you the destination of your gift, along with information about Operation Christmas Child in that country. If your boxes go to more than one country, you will receive more than one e-mail.

Special Note—The unique barcode on the label is scanned during the shipment process. Covering it with tape or damaging it could affect scanning. In the event that your label is ripped or separated from the gift in the process of shipping, it may prevent us from tracking the gift.

BUILD A BOX ONLINE

We know life can get pretty busy. But if you simply don't have time to shop and pack a shoebox yourself, you can still help change a child's life through Operation Christmas Child. We've created a process where you can build a box for a boy or girl online. You can customize your shoebox gift by selecting gifts from our list of items and adding a personal letter and photo. Your $30 donation will be used to build and send a box, to share the love of Jesus Christ.

GIFT A BOX ONLINE

Give a friend, family member, or coworker the opportunity to build a box. Donate the amount and we'll send an e-mail invitation to them so they can participate.

FAMILY DAY

An OCC event held at selected Processing Centers where families can come and get a behind-the-scenes look. Children experience how to pack and inspect a box, and learn about *The Greatest Journey* (TGJ). Parents appreciate the exposure it gives to children, encouraging them to develop a heart of service to God.

THE GREATEST JOURNEY

The follow-up discipleship course offered to shoebox recipients.

FULL CIRCLE SPEAKER

The full circle speaker is a child recipient of a shoebox gift who has been saved and speaks of his/her personal experiences about how OCC through the shoebox ministry has changed his/her life.

References

Stories are based on Samaritan's Purse Ministry Newsletters, Annual Reports, OCC Special Reports, ministry archives, books authored by Franklin Graham, or from personal interviews and personal experiences.

Below are the titles where stories were adapted:

Rebel with a Cause (Thomas Nelson, 1995)

Miracle in a Shoebox (Thomas Nelson, 1995)

Living Beyond the Limits (Thomas Nelson, 1998)

The Name (Thomas Nelson, 2002)

A Wing and a Prayer (Thomas Nelson, 2005)

Below are songs that are mentioned in the text:

"God on the Mountain" words and music by Tracy G. Dartt

"Jesus Loves Me" by Anna B. Warner

"Jesus Loves the Little Children" by George F. Root (1820–1895)